E

"We often act as though we are at the mercy of a given economic system. Vinny unlocks our minds and monetary constraints, reminding us we are in control in this excellent and thought-provoking read."

– Savannah Peterson, Founder, Savvy Millennial

"Economics is not a discipline to which we are beholden, but one which we have the opportunity to bend to our will, to create better lives for ourselves and our children. *Unlocking the Labor Cage* offers an opportunity to do just that."

– Taylor Pearson, Author, End of Jobs

"Vinny Tafuro offers a useful reminder that all economics is manmade. What is today considered 'economic gospel' was once just as provocative an idea as the proposal he offers…"

– Joe Tankersley, Futurist

"…a well-developed argument for re-configuring capitalism by shifting the model of the value-creation… to the unlimited capacity model of human talent and imagination."

– Nadine Cino, CEO, Tyga-Box

"Vinny Tafuro reminds us that the whole point of collective rule-making is the betterment of society. May his wit and wisdom ring trough the halls of legislatures and court rooms."

– Brent Britton, Managing Partner, de la Peña & Holiday LLP

ABOUT THE AUTHOR

Vinny Tafuro is a visionary thinker, writer, entrepreneur, communications theorist, and economist. Author of two books, *Corporate Empathy* and *Unlocking the Labor Cage*, he is a pioneering advocate for the twenty-first century economy that is disrupting society's most rigid institutions and beliefs.

His economic theories explore the societal and economic shifts being catalyzed by corporations as a result of technology, corporate personhood, and evolving human cognition.

He is the founder and president of Conscious Capitalism Florida, whose purpose is to seek out and connect the role models of Florida's conscious business community.

Tafuro presents to organizations, corporations, and colleges on a variety of engaging topics both professionally and through community organizations. He enjoys an active and blended professional, academic, and personal life, selecting challenging projects that offer opportunities for personal and professional growth.

Unlocking the Labor Cage

Capitalism in the Twenty-First Century

And Other Timely Essays

VINNY TAFURO

Copyright © 2016 Vinny Tafuro

All rights reserved.

ISBN: 1518610005
ISBN-13: 978-1518610004

Cover photo courtesy of NASA under public domain. Essays by Andrew Carnegie (1889) and John Maynard Keynes (1930) published under public domain.

To my mother and father. Thank you.

CONTENTS

ACKNOWLEDGMENTS

AUTHOR'S NOTE

PREFACE   1

INTRODUCTION   3

SECTION I: Technology, Labor and Empathy   5
Technological Unemployment
A False Reality
Eight-Hours Labour
Embracing Change
Evolving Empathy
The Industrialist Gospel

SECTION II: Cold War and Consumerism   13
The Cold War
Consumerism
Gross Domestic Product (GDP)
The Dismal Science

SECTION III: Globalize and Digitize   18
Globalization
Digitization
Evaporation
The Neural Economy

SECTION IV: Expiring Ideas   22
Economic Possibilities of Us
Education's Broken Contract
Keynesian Economics Revisited
The Gold Cage
The Dumbest Idea in the World
The Labor Cage
Curtain Call

SECTION V: You Can Change It   32
Stakeholder Orientation
Disrupting the Education Crisis
Corporate Cash Reserves
User Generated Content
University Fellowships
Hacking Economics

CONCLUSION   41
Capitalism in the Twenty-First Century

WORKS CITED   45

GOSPEL OF WEALTH   49
by Andrew Carnegie, 1889 (Public Domain)

ECONOMIC POSSIBILITIES FOR OUR GRANDCHILDREN   63
by John Maynard Keynes, 1930 (Public Domain)

CORPORATE EMPATHY   75
by Vinny Tafuro, 2012

ACKNOWLEDGMENTS

The publishing of *Unlocking the Labor Cage* marks another transition between stages in a continuing journey for myself and the growing circle of people who have contributed to what has become my life's work. The four years since publishing *Corporate Empathy* have been the most rewarding and challenging period of my life and it has only been through the support of others that I not only survive, but am emerging evermore centered. The following words of appreciation only just begin to express the deep gratitude I have for everyone who has touched my life in some way and made this work possible.

There is no way to appreciate enough the love and support of one's parents, with mine it is no different. My mother and father, each in their own distinct ways, have helped me to remain sane and healthy throughout the writing of this book. The support and care of my mother following my diagnosis with Type 1 Diabetes (T1D) in November 2013 allowed me to build a foundation for my, now, daily trial to maintain long-term focus on my health. So many people helped me adapt to life with T1D. I consider my diagnosis a gift – one that ensures I remain mindful of my wellbeing; that provides me a window into life with a chronic disease.

I cannot even begin to express my appreciation and love for Stephanie Street and her contribution to my life. Stephanie continues to inspire me in new ways as life unfolds before me. Stephanie's appreciation for just being, our quiet togetherness and our long discussions about meaning have forever changed me. Stephanie inspired me to return to academia armed with confidence that it was a place I could both positively influence and be influenced by.

I am grateful to The University of Tampa for providing an environment where this idea could evolve naturally over time. I would like to thank Stephanie Tripp, PhD; David Bechtold, PhD; Susan Steiner PhD; Rebecca White, PhD;

Christopher Boulton, PhD and Gregg Perkins for their contributions to this project. I must especially recognize the contributions of Dr. Tripp and Dr. Bechtold for providing invaluable direction for my research.

I want to also thank the friends and associates who have contributed in various ways to this project. Summer Cunningham, PhD and Sacha Greer, PhD for offering suggestions on structure and purpose. Paul Daigle for your early encouragement to "Never Bow Down" and suggestion to find the words of Robert F. Kennedy. My American Advertising Federation family, especially Wally Snyder who I consider a close friend and mentor, and the growing family of Conscious Capitalism practitioners who share the belief that *Everybody Matters* and it is the responsibility of business to care.

To those friends and associates not named, I am deeply grateful to all those who have become the connective tissue through which this theory will expand. Maria Popova so beautifully states, "that creative culture is woven of these invisible threads of goodwill between people who believe in one another and art is carried on the wings of this kinship." I am eternally indebted to the universe for providing so many people along my journey willing to share our belief that the world we live in is full of opportunity and that we are all involved in bringing great and transformative change to all of Earth's inhabitants.

AUTHOR'S NOTE

We hold these truths to be self-evident, that all [beings] are created equal, that they are endowed by their Creator with certain unalienable Rights, that among these are Life, Liberty and the pursuit of Happiness.
                                                  –Declaration of Independence

    The publishing of *Unlocking the Labor Cage* is the culmination of four years of observation, exploration and research into our economic past and present. By nature, *Unlocking the Labor Cage* is positioned as an argument and proposal in support of an economic theory. However, we are already traveling quickly down this road, under the guidance of metrics and isolated institutions not capable of recognizing or navigating it.

    Following the introduction of the Internet and globalization, the explosive growth of User Generated Content (UGC) has dramatically magnified the massive deficiencies of Gross Domestic Product (GDP) as an indicator of economic wellbeing. GDP merely measures the output of labor and capital. Whereas today, the age-old conflict between labor and capital is superficial. Fiat currency and technological advances have supplied both in excess, leaving us to solve a new equation: quantification and compensation of all human value creation.

    By "unlocking the labor cage" the free market is able to employ idle capital in any desirable and productive venture. While the proposal provided herein is acutely focused, the vast potential for it to create exponential wealth in our data driven society is limited only by our own creativity and the capacity of our evolving metrics. The long term societal impacts of unlocking the labor cage are scantily imaginable today and this period will be recognized as one of the most transformative periods in human history.

    Similar to feudalism's restraints as we left the agricultural age, our society is currently held captive by government and academic bureaucracies created for an industrial age. Our security, health, wellbeing, creativity and even our capacity to produce and innovate are all negatively impacted by the restraints of dated philosophies. Einstein is often quoted as saying, "We cannot solve the problems using the same kind of thinking we used when we created them." Our economic challenges today are no different. Expecting existing bureaucracies to solve today's economic challenge would be akin to the signers of the Declaration of Independence having instead offered a "Declaration of Mediation" to the King of England.

We must unlock the labor cage for value creating people everywhere to live their lives with liberty and in the pursuit of fulfillment.

No law can change how human beings evaluate the creation of value in society. Only culture can.

PREFACE

Those who are called philosophers, or men of speculation, whose trade it is not to do any thing, but to observe every thing, and who, upon that account, are often capable of combining together the powers of the most distant and dissimilar objects in the progress of society.

– Adam Smith

As illustrated in my book, *Corporate Empathy*, capitalism is maturing. While corporations increasingly find purpose and operate with passion, governments and non-profits struggle to remain relevant and solvent. Sustainable business, social enterprise and millennial entrepreneurs are destroying the walls that separate traditional institutions. When corporations fully capitalize on the economic reality that being profitable can simultaneously be good for people and the planet, the funding – and need – for bloated regulation and inefficient philanthropy will shrink.

The computer revolution and digitization has profoundly influenced almost every aspect of our daily lives. Nearly every product, service and institution has been disrupted by technology. However, economic theory has remained largely unchanged by this massive digital revolution. Economists have successfully insulated themselves through the promotion of industrial age beliefs that disregard modern reality. Economists have hidden behind the respect given the philosophical giants of economic theory, without stepping back themselves, to take a philosophical look at human society at large.

To navigate our current societal shift, we must step back and look at the previous one. Robert Heilbroner noted in 1953, that from our industrial transition away from an agricultural society, emerged "two great protagonists of the capitalist drama: worker and capitalist," leaving the feudal-era landlord "relegated to a minor position in society." Similarly, today as digitization mercilessly displaces the worker, our capitalist drama has given rise to a new protagonist: information. To understand the role that information plays in capitalism today, we must examine how economics evaluates value creation and circulates capital.

Fortunately, the principles to guide us have been available since the early half of the last century. The industrialists and philosophers of the turn of the twentieth century laid the foundation for *Unlocking the Labor Cage*, which combines "together the powers of the most distant and dissimilar objects in the progress of society" for the twenty-first century.

INTRODUCTION

Society today is in transition between two significantly different periods of human development. Similar to our transitions through the agricultural and industrial ages, our new age of information is challenging our societal operating system. The agricultural age did away with the individual's need to hunt and gather as we domesticated plants and animals. The industrial age did away with the individual's need to produce and barter as division of labor and commerce pooled resources creating an economic operating system based on capital and labor.

Our new emerging age, often and incorrectly referred to as the technology age, is a time of rapid technological advances in communications and data processing that is exponentially increasing the speed that we are able to process, share and store information. The "knowledge" or "information" age is far more descriptive considering "technology" has been ever-present, beginning with primitive stone tools. While the technological developments of the previous age are creating this new societal reality, it is not technology that will define the new age.

The transition is causing suffering as the threshold of our economic operating system is breached. For over three hundred years' philosophers Adam Smith, Karl Marx and John Maynard Keynes among others, have identified our "economic problem" as the need for civilized society to provide for itself. Keynes' 1930 prediction that we would soon solve the "economic problem" is coming to fruition along with the hardships he foresaw as well. Unprecedented technological unemployment and a staggering education debt bubble are two significant symptoms and opportunities of this transition. Keynes wrote that "we have been expressly evolved by nature-with all our impulses and deepest instincts-for the purpose of solving the economic problem. If the economic problem is solved, mankind will be deprived of its traditional purpose." As we solve the economic problem of production we must evolve our economic operating system to accommodate a more self reflective society that values knowledge and production in a similar manner. No longer can education be considered a luxury or means to an end. Investment in human intelligence must be on par with our investment in artificial intelligence.

Unlocking the Labor Cage explores how information age technologies are providing corporations with an aggressive, holistic, and fiscally sound opportunity to lead our way into the new age. The companies best positioned to capitalize on these opportunities are part of an industry already applying immense pressure on a dated economic operating system for over four decades.

We are currently caged by the idea that only labor provides compensable value in society and this book hacks at that belief. By *Unlocking the Labor Cage*, we remove obstacles that act as incentives for the status quo and hold back innovation. By *Unlocking the Labor Cage*, we remember that economics is one of the humanities. By *Unlocking the Labor Cage*, we unlock the human potential to evolve society through imagination, creativity and innovation.

SECTION I: TECHNOLOGY, LABOR AND EMPATHY

Technological Unemployment

One of the greatest improvements that has been made upon this machine, since it was first invented, was in this manner the discovery of a boy who wanted to save his own labour.

– Adam Smith

It might seem that technological unemployment would be a new phenomenon born of the information age's exponential growth of technology. However, it is actually a term that dates back to 1928 where the term first appeared in *The New Republic* on February 8 in an untitled article by Sumner Slichter (Woirol). Prior to Slichter coining the term, the article "Will New Machines Cause [an] Unemployment Crisis?" by Leland Olds and *The New Republic* editorial "Victims of the Machine" were both published in 1927 (Woirol). Throughout the early 20th century unemployment resulting from increased productivity was the subject of active discussion among economists, elected officials, and business leaders.

Prior to 1927 the effects of technological unemployment

can be identified by the labor movement described as Luddism which survives today as a term "commonly associated with opposition to new technology" (Archer, 42). At the turn of the eighteenth century new machines for textile production were displacing workers and lowering wages. The term Luddism comes from textile machine breaking in Nottinghamshire where the legendary Ned Ludd and the Luddism movement began in 1811. The movement became so destructive that by 1812 the Frame Breaking Act and the Malicious Damage Act made "machine breaking" a crime punishable by death (Archer, 49). Machine breaking as a manner of industrial protest was prevalent throughout the early nineteenth century and by some considered primitive and vandalistic. Archer concludes however, based on other research, that it was selective and controlled and resulted in a working-class movement by the 1830s desiring permanent and organized associations and unions.

Among the earliest goals of newly organized workers was improving the ratio of time worked to time available for leisurely activity.

A False Reality

The author attacks 'one of the oldest fallacies of popular economics' – the view that improvements in methods of production are undesirable, since they increase unemployment.

– A. M. Lester, 1934

In his 1934 article "The Problem of Technological Unemployment", A. M. Lester argues that the depression years following the 1929 crash and post-war economic situation was renewing a popular economic fallacy that improvements in technology lead to unemployment. In the article Lester defends the notion that over long periods of time technological advances and increases in productivity are highly desirable and socially beneficial. Instead of technological advances, Lester lays the blame for unemployment on the economic system itself. The economic system promotes overproduction in the name of keeping people employed while harvested grains are burned and cotton crops ploughed instead of harvested simply to keep prices at desirable levels. At the same time there can be under consumption and poverty because those without employment cannot afford the grains that are offered.

Lester continues on the subject of mechanization and unemployment, calling the fallacy a "great and serious source of evil". He stated, that if the relationship between the two were in fact direct, society should have twenty million unemployed instead of two million and that the standard of living should have remained at the same level as a century earlier. Instead of technology, improper management of the monetary system and balancing imports and exports is a greater cause of unemployment and falsely blaming technology allows the further mismanagement of these real causes. Lester concludes with the following:

The industry of the world is advancing and progressing still, in spite of ignorant opposition and criticism, in spite of much unwise political interference and a recent vast waste in national separatism. But all those who have the future of the human race at heart cannot help being impatient when the unnecessary obstacles are put in the road. There are quite enough difficulties to be faced without the recrudescence of a century-old fallacy in the astonishing guise of a serious economic argument.

The reality today is that our challenges are nearly identical to those described by Lester over 80 years ago. It is not our technological advances, but rather the complete failure of our economic operating system to become innovative and adaptive that is the root of our challenges.

Eight-Hours Labour

The really efficient laborer will be found not to crowd his day with work, but will saunter to his task surrounded by a wide halo of ease and leisure. There will be a wide margin for relaxation to his day. He is only earnest to secure the kernels of time, and does not exaggerate the value of the husk... Those who work much do not work hard.
– Henry David Thoreau, 1842

As early as 1817 Welsh factory owner Robert Owen envisioned the use of an eight-hour work day and coined the slogan "Eight hours labour, Eight hours recreation, Eight hours rest" as a way for workers to have a balanced life (Cahill, 1). However it is the stonemasons of Australia who claim to be the first labor group to win the eight-hour work day. Until the 1850s the skilled workers of Australia generally worked 10 hours per day during the week and eight hours on Saturday for a 58 hour work week. Working fewer hours and having control over one's life was a radical proposition for the time and considered by factory employers and the State as an attack on wealth production and taxes. According to Cahill, it was further problematic because it was believed that if workers had additional personal time "they might be out doing other things like thinking, improving themselves with reading, education and discussion, socializing, enjoying life, and maybe organizing and challenging the status quo" (Cahill, 1).

The Stonemasons were able to drive their movement because they were skilled craftsman proud of their trade and organized so that untrained and unskilled workers could not easily replace them. In August 1855 stonemasons in Australia issued ultimatums stating they would begin working eight-hour days in six months time. However in Sydney, workers on two churches decided to go on strike early, winning the eight-hour day which was celebrated October 1, 1855. Workers on a public works project in Melbourne went on strike in April 1856 to march on the Parliament House and won the eight-hour day there. In 1903 the Eight-Hour Day monument funded by the city of Melbourne was completed and stands today at the corner of Russell and Victoria streets outside the Melbourne Trades Hall.

Embracing Change

Business as a mere money-making game was not worth giving much thought to and was distinctly no place for a man who wanted to accomplish anything.

– Henry Ford

One of the best examples of an American innovator embracing technological advances and the eight-hour workday as well as respecting labor is Henry Ford, who in 1913 introduced the moving assembly line to his manufacturing process. The assembly line proved tremendously efficient and allowed the company to surpass the production levels of competitors and make vehicles more affordable. The following year Ford doubled the average employee's wage to $5 a day and reduced the workday from nine to eight hours. The changes were reported in the newspapers as a tremendous gesture of goodwill but were really just smart decisions about the role of business within society. The increased wage was enough for his workers to afford to buy the cars they were producing and the reduction to eight-hour shifts allowed production to run in three shifts around the clock, further increasing production levels. The new policies helped improve standards for all American workers which helped to spark the emergence of the American middle class as improved wages and a standard workday were adopted across American industry. Ford's success with blending the management of technology and labor to improve the situation of both employer and employee provides strong support to Lester's argument about the fallacy of technological unemployment.

Evolving Empathy

From the hour of their birth, some are marked out for subjection, others for rule... Whereas the lower animals cannot even apprehend a principle; they obey their instincts. And indeed the use made of slaves and of tame animals is not very different

– Aristotle

Unfortunately, the expansion of industrial growth and technological innovation outpaced our simultaneously evolving expectations of human rights. Worker safety was often an afterthought or even ignored depending on the motivations of the employer. While employers like Ford used efficiency and the division of labor to improve worker conditions while raising productivity, others allowed working conditions so poor that tragedy would strike.

Three years prior to Ford's introduction of the $5 paid day one of the worst labor tragedies in American history occurred. On March 25, 1911 at the Triangle Shirtwaist Factory in New York City a fire broke out on the ninth floor of the factory killing 146 immigrant workers. The tragedy placed poor working conditions in the spotlight of society and led to a number of changes in regulation. The Factory Investigating Commission (FIC) was formed just three months later and charged with investigating safety and working conditions across the state. The following year New York passed eight bills, proposed by the FIC, which in it's first year of activity, heard 222 witnesses, examined conditions in 1,836 factories in 20 different industries, and produced 3,000 pages of testimony. The bills covered conditions such as safety and sanitation, the work of new mothers, rest periods, child labor and hours of work as well as injuries sustained on the job (Cornell University).

Prior to World War II policies toward organized labor in the United Sates mostly considered the practice illegal. In 1842 a Massachusetts court decided that the mere existence of a worker organization was not itself illegal however, the specific acts of the organization could still be illegal which remained until the 1930s. Policy shifted towards providing ways for workers to organize along with protection for those organizations and workers and was embodied by the Wagner Act, more specifically known as the National Labor Relations Act of 1935 (Gallaway).

Poor labor conditions are often credited to an overly simplistic economic theory that over emphasizes profit maximization and where unionization is considered an opposing force to good business. In reality the treatment of workers is more directly linked to the progression of general human rights. While the industrial revolution catapulted our technological capabilities it simultaneously exposed how primitive our expectation of human rights was. For example, many early American industrialists lived through the Civil War era - a time when owning another human being was legal. Additionally America was the first modern republic with no separation of nobility from the peasant class. For many employers of the time placing equal value on all human lives was a new idea.

While individual employers have varied personal motivations and varying levels of empathy for workers, the treatment of workers overall has improved over time. The overall result similar to Lester's argument about technological progress, is that as our human rights expectations improve, so does our treatment of workers regardless of obstacles. From the time of Aristotle, humans have evolved to empathize with increasing larger segments of the population. Ford improved worker conditions not as a result of regulation or unions but due to his own morality and empathy for workers as partners in business (Ford).

The Industrialist Gospel

The man who dies thus rich dies disgraced.

– Andrew Carnegie

One of the most profoundly impactful industrialists, Andrew Carnegie, was additionally a respected philosopher and philanthropist, having written much in his lifetime. While Carnegie and similarly John D Rockefeller and Ford are most commonly remembered for their business practices, today's most innovative entrepreneurs have dug deep into the lives of these men through their writings. One essay of surging importance today is, "The Gospel of Wealth" written by Carnegie in 1889.

Carnegie believed that the wealthy winners of capitalism were "but a trustee for the poor; entrusted for a season with a great part of the increased wealth of the community" for the purpose of administering that wealth for the improvement of society. Having credited access to information for his success, Carnegie said, "The treasures of the world which books contain were opened to me at the right moment. The fundamental advantage of a library is that it gives nothing for nothing. Youths must acquire knowledge themselves." This belief in the power of information prompted Carnegie to build over 2,500 libraries.

Inspired by "The Gospel of Wealth," today's wealthiest entrepreneurs like Bill Gates and Warren Buffett have taken "The Giving Pledge" and given rise to a new crop of entrepreneurs like Sean Parker and Mark Zuckerberg. These newest "trustees" for the poor, have committed to dedicating a majority of their wealth to philanthropy, while simultaneously modernizing Carnegie's methods through targeted philanthropic social enterprises. Carnegie concluded that obedience to this "true Gospel concerning Wealth" would "some day solve the problem of the Rich and the Poor, and to bring 'Peace on earth, among men Good-Will.'"

SECTION II: COLD WAR AND CONSUMERISM

Practical men who believe themselves to be quite exempt from any intellectual influence, are usually the slaves of some defunct economist.
– John Maynard Keynes, 1930

    While the industrial age had been the domain of philosophers and industrialists, post WWII society was dominated by the economist; a curious academic subspecies of philosopher concerned primarily with the economic activities of society. While simultaneously denigrating philosophy and lacking entrepreneurial instincts, economists for much of the last century promoted theories that lacked depth and metrics that allow for a holistic understanding of societal wellbeing.

The Cold War

We must guard against the acquisition of unwarranted influence, whether sought or unsought, by the military industrial complex.
– Dwight D. Eisenhower, 1961

The massive production efforts and men and women needed to support the war effort and win World War II are widely credited for ending the Great Depression in the United States (Woirol 491). Despite warnings of pending unemployment when the war ended in 1945, the federal government abruptly ended its massive wartime production efforts within about a year (Gallaway 206). Instead of suffering from unemployment and a poor economy, the United States and Soviet Union emerged as two world superpowers with competing economic systems of capitalism and communism that became engaged in a 40 year Cold War. Instead of direct combat, the two sides engaged in numerous other competitive enterprises that bolstered nationalism, inspired technological innovation, and grew economies. The heavy financial investment spurred by strong nationalism quickly advanced innovations during this period easily allowing newly created jobs to replace those lost to new technology. In addition to explosive job growth in engineering, science, and medicine, the military industrial complex grew as well to support the Cold War.

Consumerism

Our enormously productive economy demands that we make consumption our way of life, that we convert the buying and use of goods into rituals, that we seek our spiritual satisfactions, our ego satisfactions, in consumption.

— Victor Lebow, 1955

While massive technological unemployment was occurring in American industry due to robotic automation and constantly improving process efficiencies, the losses were quickly absorbed in the rapidly growing consumer product and service economy. Consumerism as a solution to maintaining our postwar economy was branded and sold as the new American Dream. The foundation of consumerism was described in detail by marketing consultant Victor Lebow in "Price

Competition in 1955" published by the *Journal of Retailing*.

Lebow understood that creating a desire amongst Americans for consumption would create an ever growing economy, requiring that things be "consumed, burned up, worn out, replaced, and discarded at an ever increasing pace." Television at the time was expanding quickly through American households where Lebow saw opportunities to influence perceptions in an unprecedented manner. Television he concludes captivates an audience with the "most intensive indoctrination" and operates on the entire family. To further incite consumptive desires, Lebow points to the host of Walt Disney products, identifying franchise merchandising, where "an important name or brand is licensed for use on the products of noncompeting manufacturers'" as a strategy that "will play an even greater role than it does now."

To ensure the success of consumerism, Lebow concludes that there "must be an extension of consumer credit and installment selling." For better or worse, our modern consumer economy is a living testament of the successful adoption of Lebow's proposal.

Gross Domestic Product (GDP)

The welfare of a nation can, therefore, scarcely be inferred from a measurement of national income

– Simon Kuznets

Gross Domestic Product (GDP), originally developed as Gross National Product (GNP), is a measurement of national income. First described in a report by economist Simon Kuznets in *National Income*, at the request of the U.S. Congress in 1934, GDP/GNP is a broad quantitative measure of a nation's overall economic activity. It specifically represents the monetary value of all goods and services provided in exchange for compensation over a specified period of time. GDP takes into consideration absolutely no other measurement of societal value.

Economic growth driven by the Cold War and consumerism, however, caused economists to increasingly promote GDP as the sole indicator of America's economic and social wellbeing. Beginning with Kuznets' own warning, GDP has been criticized throughout the last century for its singular focus and complete inability to account for the true complexity of a society's welfare. In 1968 U.S. Senator Robert F. Kennedy pointed this out when he said that GNP counts "everything, in short, except that which makes life worthwhile." His address to the University of Kansas illustrates beautifully the extreme limitations of GDP.

Too much and for too long, we seemed to have surrendered personal excellence and community values in the mere accumulation of material things. Our Gross National Product, now, is over $800 billion dollars a year, but that Gross National Product - if we judge the United States of America by that - that Gross National Product counts air pollution and cigarette advertising, and ambulances to clear our highways of carnage. It counts special locks for our doors and the jails for the people who break them. It counts the destruction of the redwood and the loss of our natural wonder in chaotic sprawl. It counts napalm and counts nuclear warheads and armored cars for the police to fight the riots in our cities. It counts Whitman's rifle and Speck's knife, and the television programs which glorify violence in order to sell toys to our children. Yet the gross national product does not allow for the health of our children, the quality of their education or the joy of their play. It does not include the beauty of our poetry or the strength of our marriages, the intelligence of our public debate or the integrity of our public officials. It measures neither our wit nor our courage, neither our wisdom nor our learning, neither our compassion nor our devotion to our country, it measures everything in short, except that which makes life worthwhile. And it can tell us everything about America except why we are proud that we are Americans.

– Robert F. Kennedy, University of Kansas, March 18, 1968

The Dismal Science

If economists could manage to get themselves thought of as humble, competent people, on a level with dentists, that would be splendid!
– John Maynard Keynes

Economics is often referred to as the "dismal" science because a seemingly "inescapable element of economics is human misery." This label was coined by Thomas Carlyle, a Scottish writer and philosopher in the nineteenth century, because economics "didn't offer a hearty defense of slavery." However, "the right etymology turns that interpretation on its head. In fact, it aligns economics with morality, and against racism, rather than with misery, and against happiness." (Thompson).

The severe limitations of our economic operating system are in desperate need of an upgrade. For too long economists have been empowered to influence society with incomplete and deficient tools. While understandable that economists prefer to deal with tangible numbers, they have conveniently hidden the faults of their own sloth in convenient "catch-all" concepts like externality, greed, and growth.

We know today that externalities, such as pollution and child labor, place a heavy toll on society; that people are driven by empathy and passion not by greed and that constant economic growth through militarism and consumerism is not only a dumb idea, it cannot be sustained indefinitely. The dismal science must find enlightenment. In a global world of big data and deep metrics, today's economists can no longer hide the shortcomings of their profession.

SECTION III: GLOBALIZE AND DIGITIZE

Globalization

The 1989 removal of the Berlin Wall signaled the final days of the Soviet Union and its communist system, which collapsed under the weight of its own economic and political deficiencies just three years later. Without a shot being fired the Cold War ended abruptly, leaving the United States as a single world superpower. The United States economy surged in the 1990s through continued technological innovation and globalization.

New communication advances allowed globalization in numerous industries with corporations quickly discovering that using cheap foreign labor was a simple way to lower costs through domestic layoffs while increasing stock returns to shareholders. This began with manufacturing jobs going to China and spread throughout the customer service and technical support sectors as call centers sprang up across India. In addition to the lost jobs many Americans were further insulted by the level of support received from American companies that answered their phone calls from a foreign country.

Beginning in the 1990s, the Internet and real-estate bubbles that came and burst in succession generated economic wealth and continued the growth of American GDP, again absorbing countless jobs being displaced by technology. Since the 2008 global financial crisis, for the first time since the Great Depression, there has been sustained unemployment. While corporate profits surge, a massive wealth gap is threatening economic and societal stability. Companies continue to eliminate jobs through efficiency increases and continued technological innovation.

Digitization

Digitization is creating a second economy that's vast, automatic, and invisible -- thereby bringing the biggest change since the Industrial Revolution.

– W. Brian Arthur

The dramatic loss of jobs digitization is causing today prompts most economists, policy makers, and even business leaders to blindly look with hope to past performance. The widely accepted assumption is that with large investments in science and technology that jobs will be replaced through continued technological innovation. Over the past few years the subjects of Science Technology Engineering and Math have been compressed into the academic term "STEM" and are being over emphasized as the solution to replace all of our evaporating jobs. While focusing on computer sciences and engineering will certainly alleviate some of the pressure of technological unemployment, addressing the true vastness of our challenges will require far more creative ideas.

Evaporation

The rate at which technology is advancing today is nearly inconceivable. Just a few years ago self driving cars looked a long way off and voice recognition was pretty unreliable. Computer algorithms are being developed to replace increasingly more complex jobs. While there is common awareness that many low wage jobs are disappearing what is less understood is the impact technology is having or will soon have on a much broader variety of professions.

One now obvious area of impact is in the field of law. For the latter half of the last century, earning a law degree has been a safe haven of well compensated and stable employment. Because of high regulation and education requirements lawyers have been protected from things like outsourcing or competitive pricing. Corporate law especially, exploded in size to accommodate the need for armies of attorneys for "discovery" or the physical review of the infinite number of digital documents and emails associated with cases.

However, the bounty of work that computers produced is being eliminated by algorithms. A 2011 *New York Times* article, "Armies of Expensive Lawyers, Replaced by Cheaper Software" by John Markoff, provides startling examples to anyone not familiar. Where in a 1978 case nearly $2.2 million was spent to examine six million documents, in a 2011 case, under $100,000 could be spent for "e-discovery" examining 1.5 million documents. Markoff cites estimates in 2011, that one attorney could complete work previously requiring 500 and that real-life attorneys in one evaluation had been only 60 percent accurate compared to their digital replacements.

From retail cashiers, fast food workers and professional car/truck drivers to well educated professionals in the legal, finance, and medical field; no "job" is safe from automation in the coming decades. Government regulation and industry lobbying may hold off some advances as outdated organizations try to protect themselves but they will only collapse more spectacularly.

The Neural Economy

Long-term solutions will first require acknowledgement of a second economy that has different measurable metrics than the first. According to W. Brian Arthur the first economy was the result of the Industrial Revolution and was a physical system where machines multiplied the physical abilities of humans. Railroads, steel construction, and machines built what amounted to a skeletal frame and muscular system for the economy. The Internet and especially the connectivity brought on by social media has now formed a neural system for the economy where "individual machines-servers -- are like neurons, and the axons and synapses are the communication pathways and linkages that enable them to be in conversation with each other and to take appropriate action" (Arthur, 4).

Like the progress of worker rights, the neural economy is being created "slowly, quietly, and steadily" (Arthur 4) and as industrial age jobs evaporate with digitization long-term solutions must examine the very definition of what a job is.

SECTION IV: EXPIRING IDEAS

The information revolution is reversing the industrial revolution.
— Naval Ravikant, CEO and co-founder of AngelList

Economic Possibilities of Us

The considerable technological growth made possible by the Industrial Revolution combined with economic instability that was illustrated by numerous boom and bust cycles lead to a revaluation of economic theory in the 1930s. Out of the stock market crash and subsequent economic depression that followed the theories of British economist John Maynard Keynes became the leading school of thought for the time. Economic theory, beginning with Adam Smith's *Wealth of Nations*, has centered on supply and demand solving the "economic problem" of providing for all the participants of a society.

In 1930 Keynes published the "Economic Possibilities of our Grandchildren" where he allowed himself to look far into the future and theorize "what we can reasonably expect the level of our economic" lives to be in one hundred years. In the article Keynes concludes that if advances in society continue at a similar pace to what was currently being experienced, "the economic problem may be solved or be at least within sight of solution within a hundred years." He describes this idea as "startling to the imagination" and increasingly so, the longer one considers the ramifications. Keynes believed that our deepest impulses have evolved to specifically allow us to solve the economic problem and that once solved "mankind will be deprived" of its most basic purpose. Keynes dreaded the thought of loss felt by the ordinary person who would be forced to readjust the "habits and instincts" of countless generations within a few decades time.

After acknowledging the challenges of this probable outcome, Keynes begins to explore the likely benefits and even predicts how society may transition to this new economic reality. First he predicts that "it will be those peoples, who can keep alive, and cultivate into a fuller perfection, the art of life itself... who will be able to enjoy the abundance when it comes." He believed that people would view leisure much differently than his rich contemporaries.

With true leisure time to explore personal pursuits as opposed to what has evolved today into "vacation time" people would map out personal plans for productivity and improvement. To satisfy the urges of what he describes as the "old Adam" of needing to do some work to be contented, Keynes suggested that a fifteen-hour work week requiring "three hours a day is quite enough to satisfy the old Adam in most of us!"

Keynes sees a future where we are free to value the good in life over the merely useful. Where we celebrate those people who are able to show us how to take direct enjoyment from the things in life that make us human. A time when we can "return to some of the most sure and certain principles of religion and traditional virtue" - that extreme greed for wealth or material gain is a vice, that charging unreasonable interest is a crime, and that "the love of money is detestable."

Keynes closes with "but beware!" - the time of these changes was not yet upon his contemporaries and that "for at least another hundred years we must pretend to ourselves and to every one that fair is foul and foul is fair; for foul is useful and fair is not." Greed and high interest "must be our gods for a little longer still. For only they can lead us out of the tunnel of economic necessity into daylight."

Keynes' economic theories were given an expiration date by the philosopher himself – an expiration that is upon us today!

Education's Broken Contract

When they've tortured and scared you for twenty-odd years, then they expect you to pick a career.
– John Lennon

For the most of human history, education and work have been partners. Tribal leaders taught the younger generation about the world and how to provide for the tribe. Parents taught children how to till the land and provide for the family. Masters taught apprentices while both improved and practiced their trades. With the exception of nobility and clergy, education was for the purpose of learning to provide.

The invention of the printing press, subsequent industrial revolution, and the national revolutions that followed increasingly made education more widely available – for a cost – often meaning education was available only to the wealthy. However, by 1870 free elementary schools were available throughout America providing the U.S. population access to education regardless of financial standing (Paul).

Following World War II, college education expanded quickly as returning veterans attended universities with available GI Bill funds. This allowed the first large generation of Americans to receive a college education. Subsequently, the Boomer generation raised by these veterans were also expected to go to college as a requirement for good employment, and this trend has continued until only recently.

Beginning around the turn of the century, the value, necessity, and type of education one receives has become an increasingly heavy topic of debate. For the last half of the twentieth century the economy grew at a pace that was fast enough to absorb all college graduates with employment opportunities that paid salaries large enough to cover the cost of earning the degree. The social contract was that spending time in college to earn a degree, regardless of field of study, would prove that an applicant had discipline enough to be employed in a professional service.

Our social contract with our youth has been broken. Today, we pressure teens to make education decisions based on future employment opportunities when we ourselves have no certainty of what the employment future holds. We are penalizing them for an education breakdown we created. We are asking them to cater to an economic deficiency we have yet to acknowledge.

Keynesian Economics Revisited

The "Great Recession" has created an American economy with characteristics that seem unique. Corporate profits and cash reserves are at all time highs. Over 40 percent of the population has a college degree with nearly 90 percent having graduated high school (US Census). Simultaneously, underemployment is nearly 20 percent (Gallup). Student loan debt has ballooned to an economy crippling $1.2 trillion (Denhart). These circumstances along with increasing wealth disparity have caused wide civil unrest and created a gridlocked political environment incapable of providing economically viable solutions.

Fortunately, our societal challenges today do have a nearly identical parallel in the Great Depression. Instead of multinational corporations, there were affluent Americans who had not speculated and retained their wealth. While lacking formal educations, the American population had the physical skills necessary to work. Similarly, as well, underemployment reached upwards of 25 percent and scarce capital limited the economy's ability to recover. Unlike today however, economists and policy makers in the 1930s discussed and debated numerous and ground breaking ideas about how to rebuild the world economy.

As noted earlier, Keynesian economic theory developed out of the 1930s revaluation of the economic challenges of the Great Depression. In the "Economic Possibilities of our Grandchildren" Keynes, before looking into the future, stated that the economic suffering of the time was not a sign "that the epoch of enormous economic progress which characterised [SIC] the nineteenth century [was] over" but rather that the increases in technical efficiency and improvements in standard of life had "been a little too quick" and that the banking and monetary system of the world was unable to adjust quickly enough to keep up.

Keynes' two most influential ideas to improve the economic system and provide stability were to remove the constraints of the banking and financial system by abandoning the gold standard and to stimulate the economy through government spending made possible through borrowing and taxation. President Franklin D. Roosevelt in 1933 decided to implement both of Keynes' theories by eliminating the gold standard and implementing "a massive public works program to employ a portion of the idle workforce" known as the New Deal (Gorman).

While Roosevelt's initiatives did stimulate the economy, the Great Depression was arguably brought to an end only after the United States entered World War II. Despite the influence of the war on the testing of Keynes' theory, his ideas about stimulating the economy through government spending have enjoyed wide practice since.

The Gold Cage

It's a wonderful thing for our business men and our manufacturers and our unemployed to taste hope again. But they must not allow anyone to put them back in the gold cage where they've been pining their hearts out all these years.

– John Maynard Keynes

In *The Wealth of Nations* philosopher Adam Smith notes that different *"metals have been made use of by different nations for"* the purpose of trade since the times of the ancient Spartans and Romans. He continued that in the earliest times "the Romans had no coined money, but made use of unstamped bars of copper, to purchase whatever they had occasion for." Over time these rude bars evolved into coined money with gold and silver being widely used among all rich and commercial nations (Smith 40). The exploration and conquest of the New World combined with the technological advances brought on by the industrial revolution created a world economy controlled by the value of gold a nation possessed and remained as such until the early twentieth century.

Keynes' 1930s push for the elimination of the gold standard, which he referred to as the "gold cage," was a result of his belief that the world economy due to industrialization had outgrown the restraints placed on it by being tied to a tangible commodity. The gold standard was simply an extremely complex and overburdened form of barter. By eliminating the gold standard, the amount of money available could be regulated artificially and allowed to expand with the economy. This expansion subsequently prompted economists' unwise yet heavy reliance on Kuznets' earlier noted GDP as a measure of economic wellbeing.

The Dumbest Idea in the World

On the face of it, shareholder value is the dumbest idea in the world. Shareholder value is a result, not a strategy... Short-term profits should be allied with an increase in the long-term value of a company.
– Jack Welch, former CEO of General Electric

An unfortunate and overly simplistic idea for measuring the success of a corporation gained wide acceptance in the early 1970s. In a *New York Times* magazine article, economist Milton Friedman proclaimed rather myopically that the social responsibility of a business was to maximize monetary returns to the shareholders of the corporation. This extremely limiting concept has devolved into the short-term quarterly stock price focus we see on Wall Street today. Measuring maximized shareholder returns, similarly to using GDP, gives positive value to only one part of a more complex system. Things like negative environmental impacts, overall employee welfare, and even customer satisfaction are considered relatively inconsequential as long as the company increases profitability each quarter. The naïve simplicity of Friedman's beliefs about the purpose of business "obtained widespread support as the new gospel of business" due in part to his authoritative role as the leader of the Chicago school of economics and the fact that he was a front-runner for the 1976 Nobel Prize in Economics (Denning).

Other educators of the period, notably, management consultant and author Peter Drucker, offered alternative ideas. In the 1954 book *The Practice of Management*, Drucker stated that the purpose of business is to create and keep a customer. That by understanding the need to create and sustain a customer, the purpose of a business can be understood more holistically than by Friedman's definition. Having only ever been an academic, Friedman lacked an understanding of what motivates and drives individuals to launch companies, create innovative technologies, and disrupt the status quo.

Prior to Friedman and Drucker, Henry Ford had already illustrated the value of Drucker's philosophy by investing in his employees and compensating them well enough to become customers. Paying higher wages to employees did not lower the profits available to shareholders. Higher wages actually expanded the entire revenue pie for all stakeholders by creating customers where there previously had been few. Relatively high wages throughout most of the last century is what allowed America's economy to grow and the country's middle class to participate in the consumption cycle that had become the basis of our economy.

The Labor Cage

The idea that we repeat ourselves and we specialize and we pigeonhole ourselves is a modern invention created through the specialization of labor and the industrial revolution. Hopefully as more and more people move up Maslow's Hierarchy of Needs we're going to be able to define ourselves much more loosely.

– Naval Ravikant

The earliest divisions of labor, as observed by Smith, began our human journey towards a modern society that as Keynes foretold would eventually solve the "economic problem" of producing abundance and provide "freedom from pressing economic cares" for all. To achieve such a monumental goal society has relied on the compensation of labor as it assists in production, guided by Smith's "invisible hand" and our own evolving societal expectations of human rights.

Historically, advances in technology displacing labor have subsequently increased the need for labor. That period of expansion is over. Like the feudal-era landlord, the laborer has been "relegated to a minor position in society." This reality has left our economic system in a destructive labor cage. For example, self-driving vehicles may save over 30,000 lives annually in the USA alone while likely eliminating millions of jobs as corporations cut labor costs associated with professional human drivers and dependent services.

Idly believing that the economy will faithfully absorb these lost jobs is not only foolish but the societal changes to come will ravage traditional economic systems as technology regardless of policy or education initiatives marches forward to solve our economic problem. In the long-term we will have to expand the definition of what society considers "work" to include human endeavors other than labor and use metrics other than GDP and "hours worked" to measure the economy and compensate people for the value they produce.

Curtain Call

There was no single massive cause. The new way of life grew inside the old, like a butterfly inside a crysalis, and when the stir of life was strong enough it burst the old structure asunder. It was not great events, single adventures, individual laws, or powerful personalities that brought about the economic revolution. It was a process of spontaneous, many-sided change.

– Robert Heilbroner, 1953

As technological unemployment and productivity steadily increase, entrepreneurs are speaking out about the disappearing middle class and short-sighted economic metrics as serious risks to long economic performance and the general wellbeing of society and the planet. Larry Page and Sergey Brin of Google (Alphabet and Google X), Richard Branson of Virgin (The B Team), Howard Shultz of Starbucks (College Achievement Plan), Mark Zukerberg of Facebook (Internet.org) and John Mackey of Whole Foods (Conscious Capitalism) among many others have spoken out and started initiatives focused on addressing our most pressing concerns.

Growing numbers of entrepreneurs are deciding it is time to act and replace defunct systems and inspire creative solutions. Sean Parker who founded Napster at age 16, permanently altering the course of the music industry, recently published an open letter in the Wall Street Journal that called attention to himself and his "hacker" contemporaries. Parker, now 35 cites that a monumental shift of wealth has occurred "led by pioneers in telecommunications, personal computing, Internet services and mobile devices" that "has claimed an aggregate net worth of almost $800 billion of the $7 trillion in assets held by the wealthiest 1,000 people in the world." Parker continues, by noting that the barons of this new age have one commonality: "They are hackers."

Hackers share certain values: an antiestablishment bias, a belief in radical transparency, a nose for sniffing out vulnerabilities in systems, a desire to "hack" complex problems using elegant technological and social solutions, and an almost religious belief in the power of data to aid in solving those problems. – Sean Parker

Hacker culture is maturing along with the hackers themselves. The vast resources controlled by hackers is unprecedented. Considering their success at disrupting commercial enterprises from their garages and dorm rooms with shoestring funding, hackers are poised to successfully upend any antiquated institutions, industries and systems that refuse to evolve.

SECTION V: YOU CAN CHANGE IT

When you grow up you tend to get told that the world is the way it is and your life is just to live your life inside the world… That's a very limited life. Life can be much broader once you discover one simple fact. And that is, everything around you that you call life, was made up by people that were no smarter than you. And you can change it, you can influence it, you can build your own things that other people can use. Once you learn that you'll never be the same again.

– Steve Jobs

Society today has become hyper segmented and highly rigid. The academic Ivory Tower, The DC Beltway, and Wall Street are incapable of providing solutions to our challenges. With the exception of rebellious individuals, these institutions more often create roadblocks to innovation rather than encourage it. Our economic operating system was created by people who have passed into the pages of history. Their ideas served a different time. Entrepreneurs are the primary innovators of today's society. It is up entrepreneurs to disrupt our economic operating system.

Stakeholder Orientation

Conscious Capitalism to me has a very competitive aspect to it. It's competing to make the world a better place.
– Tom Gardner, The Motley Fool

While traditional economic theory has perpetuated the falsity of profits and greed as the single highest motivator of people and business, the world's entrepreneurs are innovating.

John Mackey and Raj Sisodia's book *Conscious Capitalism* and the Conscious Capitalism movement describe and promote business as a solution to societal challenges and provides a more holistic way to look at business. Conscious Capitalism in practice looks to balance the needs of all stakeholders to improve long-term sustained performance and "liberating the heroic spirit of business" by finding win-win-win solutions instead of tradeoffs. Richard Branson's The B Team is a non-profit initiative of global leaders who believe that the purpose of business is to be "a driving force for social, environmental and economic benefit" for the world.

In September 2015 Kickstarter founders Yancey Strickler and Perry Chen gained wide attention from the business and investment community announcing that Kickstarter had reorganized as a benefit corporation. As a benefit corporation, Kickstarter has elected to hold itself to high level of transparency while remaining a nimble and innovative for profit enterprise. The new designation will enhance the company's long term sustainability by ensuring that its mission is retained.

In 2014 Howard Shultz took one of the boldest direct steps to strengthen the middle class, increase customer loyalty and ensure continued long-term financial success for shareholders. In June, Starbucks announced the Starbucks College Achievement Plan, "making it possible for thousands of part- and full-time U.S. partners to complete a college degree." Starbucks is partnered with Arizona State University to provide full tuition reimbursement for any of 40 undergraduate degree programs delivered online – with no requirement to stay with the company. Schultz said in a statement that, "We as a company want to do something that has not been done before. That is, we want to create access to the American Dream, hope and opportunity for everybody."

Disrupting the Education Crisis

Technological unemployment and technological advances coupled with crippling student loan debt and innovative enterprises are disrupting an American higher education system that is in crisis. Federally guaranteed student loans, sky high administrative costs and deplorable adjunct teaching policies have created a wide opportunity for universities and entrepreneurs to experiment with innovative solutions to avoid a system-wide collapse.

Many college graduates find that degrees they earned are not needed to attain employment while at the same time they lack skills necessary for jobs that are available. Due to student loan availability, many recent graduates quickly return seeking graduate level degrees in the hope that they will emerge better qualified in an improved job market. This easy access to federally guaranteed loans has created a student loan debt bubble of $1.2 trillion (Denhart).

Access to unlimited federally guaranteed student loans combined with a "business mindset" in academic institutions have created an impossible situation for a majority of instructors. Like traditional companies where executive compensation soars and expanding use of part time workers reduces costs, American colleges have been increasing administrative budgets while replacing full time faculty with adjunct teaching staff. Nationally, adjuncts now account for about 70 percent of instructors and often times must travel between colleges to teach enough classes to make a living. This expansive use of part-time instructors negatively impacts students because instructors are stressed to keep uncoordinated schedules and have very little time outside of the classroom to provide support (Williams June). Additionally, adjuncts are not invited to participate or provide opportunities to influence universities through administrative and faculty meetings or other activities that help improve higher education.

The nation's top private non-profit universities are reimagining the future of higher education and actively partnering with private sector entrepreneurs and technology companies to explore new opportunities to provide education. Stanford, MIT, Duke, Harvard, Yale, Carnegie Mellon and the University of Pennsylvania for example now offer many courses through initiatives called Massive Open Online Courses (MOOCs), where full college courses are made available for free to anyone who would like to register. While these courses do not provide college credit, the course work is the same and the knowledge acquired by the student is not diminished. Companies like Coursera provide an education platform that allows universities worldwide to offer these courses.

Higher education, unlike the general economy, does not rely on one single metric to measure value and does not arbitrarily ignore metrics that are not easily quantified. In addition to traditional test scores, higher education uses peer review and evaluation to assign merit to activities that can be included in the overall assessment of student achievement. This model of assessment and cost reduction is creating an opportunity for scalable semi-self guided education that could provide high quality education for a significant segment of the population.

Corporate Cash Reserves

Often it is reported and discussed that corporations are sitting on huge cash reserves that could be used to "lower prices and create jobs" in an effort to help build the economy. While the dollar amount of $1.73 trillion is in fact enormous, Jeffrey Dorfman explained on *Forbes.com* in 2014 that at about 13 percent of overall corporate revenue the number is close to the 10 percent historic average that companies would retain. Secondly, globalization has led to about $1.1 trillion of the total being held outside of the United States to avoid a 35 percent tax on the revenues earned internationally.

There have been conversations by Congress, the President and numerous corporate executives about how to best repatriate the overseas cash reserves with no consensus on a short or long-term solution. A popular "tax holiday" option offering a reduced tax rate for repatriated funds was previously offered in 2004. While about 50% percent was brought home, the bulk "went not to research or building factories" but instead to stockholder dividend payments (Foroohar). Without a recent tax holiday, companies have not suffered a lack of domestic cash. Due to record low loan interest rates, companies that desire liquidity can borrow the cash needed at a lower cost than repatriating foreign funds. Walmart did exactly this in 2013 when it borrowed $5 billion without specific reason at a lower cost than repatriating the same amount (Dorfman).

The motivations of companies to repatriate cash reserves are far more complex as illustrated by Ebay's decision to absorb a $3 billion tax hit to repatriate $9 billion in early 2014. The company's chief financial officer, Bob Swan, said that while the company had no planned acquisitions that EBay was "an acquisitive company" and needed to "have the resources available to capitalize on targets that become available" (Bensinger). However, by the end of 2014, the purpose of the repatriation became more clear as the company announced the potential trimming of 3,000 jobs as part of a plan to spinoff PayPal as an independent company and make EBay itself an attractive target for an acquisition (Bensinger).

In *The Wealth of Nations*, Adam Smith discusses in Chapter II the evaluation of money as a segment of the economy. Smith states that the gross "revenue of any society" is computed as "the whole annual circulation of money and goods" after we "deduct the whole value of the money, of which not a single farthing can ever make any part of either" or that the "revenue of the society consists altogether in those goods, and not in the wheel which circulates them" (Smith 475). In simple terms, this means that while the accumulated cash reserves discussed above may serve potential future business functions, the money is actually just an idle resource not providing immediate measurable value of any kind to the corporation.

While wise to keep cash reserves to protect against business challenges, the current levels could be considered wasteful considering the amount of economic and market data that companies have available to predict performance. Companies today are harming their long-term performance by using outdated accounting principles in deciding how much cash to retain. Because these reserves are already removed from providing short-term value, a portion could be invested in long-term initiatives.

User Generated Content

The societal connectivity that social media and the Internet provides has created a vast and ever growing amount of data, responsible for significant unmeasured economic value. From a simple Facebook "Like" to the in-depth reviews shared on sites like Yelp and Amazon, the Internet is driven in large part by User Generated Content (UGC). The business models of companies like Facebook, Google and Amazon rest almost entirely on the generation of content by users of the services. While the value of this content to our economy is undeniable, it goes unmeasured and ignored by GDP.

In the *Second Machine Age*, by Andrew McAfee and Erik Brynjolfsson, the authors describe the conundrum that UGC poses; "user-generated content… involves unmeasured labor creating an unmeasured asset that is consumed in unmeasured ways to create unmeasured consumer surplus." UGC as a form of labor and capital is unmeasured and uncompensated, and as a corporate asset, not cultivated like traditional labor and capital. This lack of attention to such a key asset in the business model is surprising yet understandable given the flaws of current industrial age economic science.

A primary mental roadblock to simultaneously considering UGC as both "labor" and "capital" stems from the fact that industrial age labor is provided in direct exchange for capital in the form of wages. Whereas most UGC by its very nature cannot be directly compensated as labor without destroying the authenticity of the content. The lack of attention given to cultivating this essential economic asset is further limited by an industrial age mentality that human capital is easily replaced – like the parts of a machine. Industrial age work consists mostly of repetition of operations, resulting in economic metrics that treat both employees and consumers as expendable commodities to be replaced with ease.

Those economic beliefs will serve no more. UGC must be quantified and valuated as a core component of the economy. Fortunately, the knowledge age marketplace is maturing and companies are emerging to seize opportunities presented by UGC. MeSpoke, a tailored community digitally reinventing retail through mobile, uses UGC to connect consumers directly. MeSpoke users known as "Speakers" influence the popularity of brands and retailers using their own "Social Capital" to democratize the industry and motivate people to act. MeSpoke CEO, S. Khurrum Hasan recognizes UGC as the cornerstone of MeSpoke's DNA and Social Capital as a significant and undercapitalized component of the economy.

Human capital is an essential and renewable resource that drives our information age economy the same way financial capital drove the industrial age. The same care and investment priority given to a company's fiscal capital must now be extended to all human capital.

University Fellowships

While the American higher education system is headed for financial collapse, it also presents a great opportunity for investment. Most people are familiar with scholarships commonly sought by undergraduate students to cover education costs. People are less familiar however, with university fellowships that are almost exclusively reserved for academics seeking graduate or post graduate degrees. Fellowships are merit-based financial awards provided as support to graduate students seeking a post graduate degree such as a PhD. Fellowships are awarded by foundations, corporations, and universities themselves and often cover not only tuition but health insurance as well as a stipend for living expenses. Fellowships, unlike student loans, are not paid back by the student and seen as an investment in the student, the university, and the field of study.

According to the College Board, the average cost of tuition and fees for the 2014-2015 school year was $31,231 at private non-profit universities, $9,139 for state residents at public universities, and $22,958 for out-of-state residents attending public universities. The estimated average tuition for a full-time undergraduate student is $21,109 per year. The overall estimated budget for a private nonprofit four year on-campus student is $46,272, which in addition to tuition, includes room and board, books and supplies, transportation and other expenses not specified.

Hacking Economics

We as a company want to do something that has not been done before. That is, we want to create access to the American Dream, hope and opportunity for everybody.

– Howard Shultz

The education crisis and disappearing middle class are a direct result of industrial age government policy directed by industrial age economic theory. Policy makers and economists are unable to create solutions because neither group has the ability or incentive to make disruptive changes. The only stakeholder capable of creating dramatic and sustainable change are corporations. If there was any doubt to their ability, in 2014 the Supreme Court of the United States clarified that a corporate "person" has a purpose "to provide protection for human beings" and that a "corporation is simply a form of organization used by human beings to achieve desired ends." The court does not define what those desires are, appropriately leaving that to the market.

Returning to the earlier look at corporate cash reserves but focusing on the technology sector which *Forbes.com* staff writer Lauren Gensler reported in May 2015 held $690 billion, or 40 percent of the $1.73 trillion held by all U.S. non-financial companies. Gensler states that "companies like Microsoft, Cisco and Oracle have 90% or more of their cash piles abroad" to avoid taxes. Repatriating cash reserves to invest in education would eliminate the associated corporate tax burden while stimulating massive disruptive changes within the education sector and increasing access to higher education.

Just one percent of the estimated technology sector's cash reserves is $6.9 billion and of just one company, Google for example, $644 million. Estimating average tuition of $20,000 combined with a $30,000 stipend for living expenses for a total annual investment of $50,000 per student, the technology sector's one percent investment could provide 138,000 undergraduate fellowships. A one percent investment by Google alone would provide 12,880 fellowships.

While the above example quickly illustrates the enormous impact of this investment, the actual investments could be much larger. The earlier mentioned challenges created by UGC could be addressed through UGC valuation tied to fellowship contributions. This investment in human capital would be indirect and distributed through the existing merit based academic system, providing accountability. The investment would address the compensation dilemma of UGC while simultaneously nurturing UGC as a valuable and renewal company asset.

CONCLUSION

Capitalism in the Twenty-First Century

For as long as the technics of society change, no existing division of wealth is immune from attack.

– Robert Heilbroner

Unlocking the Labor Cage is the first step to reconfiguring capitalism for the twenty-first century. Contemporary economic theory restricts capitalism to three methods of currency circulation. The first and primary being the voluntary exchange of capital for labor. The second being the involuntary acquisition of capital by governments through taxation. The final being the voluntary donation of profits to charitable organizations. These are the only three options currently available. Due to technological unemployment through digitization and automation, the primary method is quickly disappearing. *Unlocking the Labor Cage* is a proposition for adding a critically needed and voluntary fourth method: The circulation of currency through voluntary private sector investment of excess corporate cash reserves into education based on the value of a corporation's user generated content.

Century-old corporate accounting practices for cash

reserves were developed in a time when business executives relied on newspapers, fax machines, the U.S. Postal Service, and hand printed accounting legers to track market conditions and company performance. Whereas today's companies are extremely nimble and have instant access to a wealth of data to make decisions and respond quickly to market conditions. Therefore, it is arguable that current levels of cash reserves are damaging not only to the performance of the company, but to all stakeholders, including shareholders.

Contemporary policy makers and economists have been unsuccessful in identifying these significant flaws in our economic system and are blindly hopeful that enough jobs will eventually be created to restore vibrancy. While the creation of jobs and new industries will certainly occur following investments in the fields of Science, Technology, Engineering, and Math, popularly known as STEM education, the basic understanding of what a "job" will be in the future must be adjusted. In our knowledge age of "big data" we must expand the definition and metrics of compensable value creation.

By investing just one percent of the technology sector's current cash reserves into unrestricted undergraduate fellowships, nearly 150 thousand students could be awarded fellowships annually. Unlike philanthropic giving or taxation these investments would be soundly based on the overall value of a company's user generated content; and the institutions receiving investments would be held accountable for student performance. However, because current tax code would identify these investments as philanthropic, corporations could repatriate funds for these investments with zero tax burden.

This upgrade to our antiquated economic operating system is just one step. A voluntary step with huge ramifications for society. A major step into a true knowledge economy. With hundreds of thousands of people able to focus on education without the need for traditional employment, upward pressure would be placed on wages. Competition for funds would place significant downward pressure on college administrative costs while incentivizing the hiring of more faculty professors. As universities refocus on education over administration the deplorable treatment of adjuncts would come to an end. Without being concerned about college's "return on investment" emphasis would return to the importance of a liberal arts degree over premature specialization. This new source of funding for education would also loosen the stranglehold of debt that has been placed on our young adults by a broken system. Furthermore, the overall cost of higher education would decline allowing even more fellowships to be offered; further expanding the societal benefits.

Funding education is just an initial step to introduce this new method of currency circulation. While user generated content is a measurable corporate asset, it's creation cannot typically be directly compensated without destroying the nature of the data. Therefore this investment in education is a timely opportunity to begin experimenting with this method as a way to cultivate future user generated content. User generated content is already quantified and monetized by the advertising industry, where according the Interactive Advertising Bureau, $27.5 billion was spent in just the first half of 2015.

Private sector adoption of this proposal is the first step to building a stronger and more sustainable economy and society. This proposal will create transactions and stimulate the economy. Similar to the argument of Victor Lebow in 1955 for our economic need for consumerism, and the use of television advertising to drive demand; the impact of this proposal will be felt throughout society and over many decades.

Once user generated content is recognized as a critical corporate asset to be actively cultivated, the opportunities for corporate accounting principles to evolve and circulate currency through an increasingly wide variety of investments becomes available. The distribution of wealth within the economy would begin to shift dramatically. This shift will reestablish a flourishing middle class, while sustaining healthy and profitable corporations; corporations, now economically enabled to adjust to the needs of a knowledge driven modern society.

WORKS CITED

Abramovitz M. Simon Kuznets (1901–1985) // The Journal of Economic History, March 1986, v.46, no.1, p. 246.

Woirol, Gregory R. "New Data, New Issues: The Origins of the Technological Unemployment Debates"
History of Political Economy. Fall2006, Vol. 38 Issue 3, p473-496. 24p

Cahill, Rowan. "The Eight Hour Day and the Holy Spirit". *Workers Online*. Labor Council of N.S.W.

Lester, A. M. "The Problem Of Technological Unemployment." Human Factors (03017397) 8.5 (1934): 180-187

Archer, John E. (2000). "Chapter 4: Industrial Protest". *Social unrest and popular protest in England, 1780–1840*. Cambridge University Press. ISBN 978-0-521-57656-7. (via Google Books)

Ford Motor Company "Henry Ford's $5-a-Day Revolution", Ford, Jan 5, 1914, accessed April 23, 2011. (via Ford website)

Cornell University website. "The Triangle Factor Fire". http://www.ilr.cornell.edu/trianglefire

Gallaway, Lowell E. "Unions, The High-Wage Doctrine, And Employment." CATO Journal 30.1 (2010): 197-213

Roger, Simon "Bobby Kennedy on GDP: 'measures everything except that which is worthwhile" *The Guardian*, May 24, 2012

Thompson, Derek "Why Economics Is Really Called 'the Dismal Science' *The Atlantic*, Dec 17, 2013

Arthur, W. Brian. "The second economy." Mckinsey Quarterly no. 4 (Dec 2011): 90-99. Business Source Complete, EBSCOhost (accessed Apr 23, 2013).

Markoff, John "Armies of Expensive Lawyers, Replaced by Cheaper Software" *New York Times*, Mar 4, 2011

Keynes, John Maynard, "Economic Possibilities for our Grandchildren" (1930)

US Census "Educational Attainment in the United States: 2013 - Detailed Tables" (via Wikipedia)

Gallup Daily: U.S. Employment (via Gallup website)

Denhart, Chris "How The $1.2 Trillion College Debt Crisis Is Crippling Students, Parents And The Economy" *Forbes website*, Aug 7, 2013

Gordon, Tom "The Complete Idiot's Guide to Economics" Penguin Group (USA) Inc. (2003)

Simon Kuznets, 1934. "National Income, 1929–1932"

Denning, Steve "The Origin Of 'The World's Dumbest Idea': Milton Friedman" *Forbes*, Jun 26, 2013

Williams June, Audrey "Adjuncts Gain Traction With Congressional Attention" *The Chronicle* Feb 3, 2014

Drucker, Peter "The Practice of Management" New York : Harper & Row, c1954.

Mui, Chunka "Will Driverless Cars Force A Choice Between Lives And Jobs?" *Forbes*, Dec 19, 2013

Vinsel, Lee "Autonomous Vehicles and the Labor Question", *Taming the American Idol*, Dec 2, 2013 (Blog)

Monroe, Paul "A cyclopedia of education (4 vol. 1911)" The MacMillan Company, 1926 (via Wikipedia)

Dorfman, Jeffrey "Dispelling The Myth of Corporate Cash Hoarding" *Forbes*, Aug 21, 2014

Foroohar, Rana "The Trillion-Dollar Homecoming" *Time* Jan 14, 2013, Vol. 181 Issue 1, p20-20. 1p.

Bensinger, Greg "EBay Absorbs $3 Billion Hit To Repatriate Foreign Cash." *Wall Street Journal – Eastern Edition* Mar 30, 2014, Vol. 263 Issue 100, pB5-B5. 1/6p.

Bensinger, Greg "EBay Mulls Thousands of Job Cuts Next Year" *Wall Street Journal (Online)*, Dec 10, 2014

THE GOSPEL OF WEALTH
Andrew Carnegie, 1889 (Public Domain)

The Problem of the Administration of Wealth

The problem of our age is the proper administration of wealth, so that the ties of brotherhood may still bind together the rich and poor in harmonious relationship. The conditions of human life have not only been changed, but revolutionized, within the past few hundred years. In former days there was little difference between the dwelling, dress, food, and environment of the chief and those of his retainers. The Indians are to-day where civilized man then was. When visiting the Sioux, I was led to the wigwam of the chief. It was just like the others in external appearance, and even within the difference was trifling between it and those of the poorest of his braves. The contrast between the palace of the millionaire and the cottage of the laborer with us to-day measures the change which has come with civilization.

This change, however, is not to be deplored, but welcomed as highly beneficial. It is well, nay, essential for the progress of the race, that the houses of some should be homes for all that is highest and best in literature and the arts, and for all the refinements of civilization, rather than that none should be so. Much better this great irregularity than universal squalor. Without wealth there can be no Mæcenas. The "good old times" were not good old times. Neither master nor servant was as well situated then as to-day. A relapse to old conditions would be disastrous to both—not the least so to him who serves—and would Sweep away civilization with it. But whether the change be for good or ill, it is upon us, beyond our power to alter, and there fore to be accepted and made the best of. It is a waste of time to criticise the inevitable.

ANDREW CARNEGIE

It is easy to see how the change has come. One illustration will serve for almost every phase of the cause. In the manufacture of products we have the whole story. It applies to all combinations of human industry, as stimulated and enlarged by the inventions of this scientific age. Formerly articles were manufactured at the domestic hearth or in small shops which formed part of the household. The master and his apprentices worked side by side, the latter living with the master, and therefore subject to the same conditions. When these apprentices rose to be masters, there was little or no change in their mode of life, and they, in turn, educated in the same routine succeeding apprentices. There was, substantially social equality, and even political equality, for those engaged in industrial pursuits had then little or no political voice in the State.

But the inevitable result of such a mode of manufacture was crude articles at high prices. To-day the world obtains commodities of excellent quality at prices which even the generation preceding this would have deemed incredible. In the commercial world similar causes have produced similar results, and the race is benefited thereby. The poor enjoy what the rich could not before afford. What were the luxuries have become the necessaries of life. The laborer has now more comforts than the landlord had a few generations ago. The farmer has more luxuries than the landlord had, and is more richly clad and better housed. The landlord has books and pictures rarer, and appointments more artistic, than the King could then obtain.

The price we pay for this salutary change is, no doubt, great. We assemble thousands of operatives in the factory, in the mine, and in the counting-house, of whom the employer can know little or nothing, and to whom the employer is little better than a myth. All intercourse between them is at an end. Rigid Castes are formed, and, as usual, mutual ignorance breeds mutual distrust. Each Caste is without sympathy for the other, and ready to credit anything disparaging in regard to it. Under the law of competition, the employer of thousands is forced into the strictest economies, among which the rates paid to labor figure prominently, and often there is friction between the employer and the employed, between capital and labor, between rich and poor. Human society loses homogeneity.

The price which society pays for the law of competition, like the price it pays for cheap comforts and luxuries, is also great; but the advantage of this law are also greater still, for it is to this law that we owe our wonderful material development, which brings improved conditions in its train. But, whether the law be benign or not, we must say of it, as we say of the change in the conditions of men to which we have referred : It is here; we cannot evade it; no substitutes for it have been found; and while the law may be sometimes hard for the individual, it is best for the race, because it insures the survival of the fittest in every department. We accept and welcome therefore, as conditions to which we must accommodate ourselves, great inequality of environment, the concentration of business, industrial and commercial, in the hands of a few, and the law of competition between these, as being not only beneficial, but essential for the future progress of the race. Having accepted these, it follows that there must be great scope for the exercise of special ability in the merchant and in the manufacturer who has to conduct affairs upon a great scale. That this talent for organization and management is rare among men is proved by the fact that it invariably secures for its possessor enormous rewards, no matter where or under what laws or conditions. The experienced in affairs always rate the MAN whose services can be obtained as a partner as not only the first consideration, but such as to render the question of his capital scarcely worth considering, for such men soon create capital; while, without the special talent required, capital soon takes wings. Such men become interested in firms or corporations using millions; and estimating only simple interest to be made upon the capital invested, it is inevitable that their income must exceed their expenditures, and that they must accumulate wealth. Nor is there any middle ground which such men can occupy, because the great manufacturing or commercial concern which does not earn at least interest upon its capital soon becomes bankrupt. It, must either go forward or fall behind: to stand still is impossible. It is a condition essential for its successful operation that it should be thus far profitable, and even that, in addition to interest on capital, it should make profit. It is a law, as certain as any of the others named, that men possessed of this peculiar talent for affair, under the free play of economic forces, must, of necessity, soon be in receipt of more revenue than can be judiciously expended upon themselves; and this law is as beneficial for the race as the others.

Objections to the foundations upon which society is based are not in order, because the condition of the race is better with these than it has been with any others which have been tried. Of the effect of any new substitutes proposed we cannot be sure. The Socialist or Anarchist who seeks to overturn present conditions is to be regarded as attacking the foundation upon which civilization itself rests, for civilization took its start from the day that the capable, industrious workman said to his incompetent and lazy fellow, "If thou dost not sow, thou shalt not reap," and thus ended primitive Communism by separating the drones from the bees. One who studies this subject will soon be brought face to face with the conclusion that upon the sacredness of property civilization itself depends—the right of the laborer to his hundred dollars in the savings bank, and equally the legal right of the millionaire to his millions. To these who propose to substitute Communism for this intense Individualism the answer, therefore, is: The race has tried that. All progress from that barbarous day to the present time has resulted from its displacement. Not evil, but good, has come to the race from the accumulation of wealth by those who have the ability and energy that produce it. But even if we admit for a moment that it might be better for the race to discard its present foundation, Individualism,—that it is a nobler ideal that man should labor, not for himself alone, but in and for a brotherhood of his fellows, and share with them all in common, realizing Swedenborg's idea of Heaven, where, as he says, the angels derive their happiness, not from laboring for self, but for each other,—even admit all this, and a sufficient answer is, This is not evolution, but revolution. It necessitates the changing of human nature itself a work of eons, even if it were good to change it, which we cannot know. It is not practicable in our day or in our age. Even if desirable theoretically, it belongs to another and long-succeeding sociological stratum. Our duty is with what is practicable now; with the next step possible in our day and generation. It is criminal to waste our energies in endeavoring to uproot, when all we can profitably or possibly accomplish is to bend the universal tree of humanity a little in the direction most favorable to the production of good fruit under existing circumstances. We might as well urge the destruction of the highest existing type of man because he failed to reach our ideal as favor the destruction of Individualism, Private Property, the Law of Accumulation of Wealth, and the Law of Competition; for these are the highest results of human experience, the soil in which society so far has produced the best fruit. Unequally or unjustly, perhaps, as these laws sometimes operate, and imperfect as they appear to the Idealist, they are, nevertheless, like the highest type of man, the best and most valuable of all that humanity has yet accomplished.

We start, then, with a condition of affairs under which the best interests of the race are promoted, but which inevitably gives wealth to the few. Thus far, accepting conditions as they exist, the situation can be surveyed and pronounced good. The question then arises,—and, if the foregoing be correct, it is the only question with which we have to deal,—What is the proper mode of administering wealth after the laws upon which civilization is founded have thrown it into the hands of the few? And it is of this great question that I believe I offer the true solution. It will be understood that fortunes are here spoken of, not moderate sums saved by many years of effort, the returns on which are required for the comfortable maintenance and education of families. This is not wealth, but only competence which it should be the aim of all to acquire.

There are but three modes in which surplus wealth can be disposed of. It call be left to the families of the decedents; or it can be bequeathed for public purposes; or, finally, it can be administered during their lives by its possessors. Under the first and second modes most of the wealth of the world that has reached the few has hitherto been applied. Let us in turn consider each of these modes. The first is the most injudicious. In monarchical countries, the estates and the greatest portion of the wealth are left to the first son, that the vanity of the parent may be gratified by the thought that his name and title are to descend to succeeding generations unimpaired. The condition of this class in Europe to-day teaches the futility of such hopes or ambitions. The successors have become impoverished through their follies or from the fall in the value of land. Even in Great Britain the strict law of entail has been found inadequate to maintain the status of an hereditary class. Its soil is rapidly passing into the hands of the stranger. Under republican institutions the division of property among the children is much fairer, but the question which forces itself upon thoughtful men in all lands is: Why should men leave great fortunes to their children? If this is done from affection, is it not misguided affection? Observation teaches that, generally speaking, it is not well for the children that they should be so burdened. Neither is it well for the state. Beyond providing for the wife and daughters moderate sources of income, and very moderate allowances indeed, if any, for the sons, men may well hesitate, for it is no longer questionable that great sums bequeathed oftener work more for the injury than for the good of the recipients. Wise men will soon conclude that, for the best interests of the members of their families and of the state, such bequests are an improper use of their means.

It is not suggested that men who have failed to educate their sons to earn a livelihood shall cast them adrift in poverty. If any man has seen fit to rear his sons with a view to their living idle lives, or, what is highly commendable, has instilled in them the sentiment that they are in a position to labor for public ends without reference to pecuniary considerations, then, of course, the duty of the parent is to see that such are provided for in moderation. There are instances of millionaires' sons unspoiled by wealth, who, being rich, still perform great services in the community. Such are the very salt of the earth, as valuable as, unfortunately, they are rare; still it is not the exception, but the rule, that men must regard, and, looking at the usual result of enormous sums conferred upon legatees, the thoughtful man must shortly say, "I would as soon leave to my son a curse as the almighty dollar," and admit to himself that it is not the welfare of the children, but family pride, which inspires these enormous legacies.

As to the second mode, that of leaving wealth at death for public uses, it may be said that this is only a means for the disposal of wealth, provided a man is content to wait until he is dead before it becomes of much good in the world. Knowledge of the results of legacies bequeathed is not calculated to inspire the brightest hopes of much posthumous good being accomplished. The cases are not few in which the real object sought by the testator is not attained, nor are they few in which his real wishes are thwarted. In many cases the bequests are so used as to become only monuments of his folly. It is well to remember that it requires the exercise of not less ability than that which acquired the wealth to use it so as to be really beneficial to the community. Besides this, it may

ANDREW CARNEGIE

fairly be said that no man is to be extolled for doing what he cannot help doing, nor is he to be thanked by the community to which he only leaves wealth at death. Men who leave vast sums in this way may fairly be thought men who would not have left it at all, had they been able to take it with them. The memories of such cannot be held in grateful remembrance, for there is no grace in their gifts. It is not to be wondered at that such bequests seem so generally to lack the blessing.

The growing disposition to tax more and more heavily large estates left at death is a cheering indication of the growth of a salutary change in public opinion. The State of Pennsylvania now takes—subject to some exceptions—one-tenth of the property left by its citizens. The budget presented in the British Parliament the other day proposes to increase the death-duties; and, most significant of all, the new tax is to be a graduated one. Of all forms of taxation, this seems the wisest. Men who continue hoarding great sums all their lives, the proper use of which for–public ends would work good to the community, should be made to feel that the community, in the form of the state, cannot thus be deprived of its proper share. By taxing estates heavily at death the state marks its condemnation of the selfish millionaire's unworthy life.

It is desirable; that nations should go much further in this direction. Indeed, it is difficult to set bounds to the share of a rich man's estate which should go at his death to the public through the agency of the state, and by all means such taxes should be graduated, beginning at nothing upon moderate sums to dependents, and increasing rapidly as the amounts swell, until of the millionaire's hoard, as of Shylock's, at least

The other half
Comes to the privy coffer of the state.

This policy would work powerfully to induce the rich man to attend to the administration of wealth during his life, which is the end that society should always have in view, as being that by far most fruitful for the people. Nor need it be feared that this policy would sap the root of enterprise and render men less anxious to accumulate, for to the class whose ambition it is to leave great fortunes and be talked about after their death, it will attract even more attention, and, indeed, be a somewhat nobler ambition to have enormous sums paid over to the state from their fortunes.

There remains, then, only one mode of using great fortunes; but in this we have the true antidote for the temporary unequal distribution of wealth, the reconciliation of the rich and the poor—a reign of harmony—another ideal, differing, indeed, from that of the Communist in requiring only the further evolution of existing conditions, not the total overthrow of our civilization. It is founded upon the present most intense individualism, and the race is projected to put it in practice by degree whenever it pleases. Under its sway we shall have an ideal state, in which the surplus wealth of the few will become, in the best sense the property of the many, because administered for the common good, and this wealth, passing through the hands of the few, can be made a much more potent force for the elevation of our race than if it had been distributed in small sums to the people themselves. Even the poorest can be made to see this, and to agree that great sums gathered by some of their fellow-citizens and spent for public purposes, from which the masses reap the principal benefit, are more valuable to them than if scattered among them through the course of many years in trifling amounts.

If we consider what results flow from the Cooper Institute, for instance, to the best portion of the race in New York not possessed of means, and compare these with those which would have arisen for the good of the masses from an equal sum distributed by Mr. Cooper in his lifetime in the form of wages, which is the highest form of distribution, being for work done and not for charity, we can form some estimate of the possibilities for the improvement of the race which lie embedded in the present law of the accumulation of wealth. Much of this sum if distributed in small quantities among the people, would have been wasted in the indulgence of appetite, some of it in excess, and it may be doubted whether even the part put to the best use, that of adding to the comforts of the home, would have yielded results for the race, as a race, at all comparable to those which are flowing and are to flow from the Cooper Institute from generation to generation. Let the advocate of violent or radical change ponder well this thought.

We might even go so far as to take another instance, that of Mr. Tilden's bequest of five millions of dollars for a free library in the city of New York, but in referring to this one cannot help saying involuntarily, how much better if Mr. Tilden had devoted the last years of his own life to the proper administration of this immense sum; in which case neither legal contest nor any other cause of delay could have interfered with his aims. But let us assume that Mr. Tilden's millions finally become the means of giving to this city a noble public library, where the treasures of the world contained in books will be open to all forever, without money and without price. Considering the good of that part of the race which congregates in and around Manhattan Island, would its permanent benefit have been better promoted had these millions been allowed to circulate in small sums through the hands of the masses? Even the most strenuous advocate of Communism must entertain a doubt upon this subject. Most of those who think will probably entertain no doubt whatever.

Poor and restricted are our opportunities in this life; narrow our horizon; our best work most imperfect; but rich men should be thankful for one inestimable boon. They have it in their power during their lives to busy themselves in organizing benefactions from which the masses of their fellows will derive lasting advantage, and thus dignify their own lives. The highest life is probably to be reached, not by such imitation of the life of Christ as Count Tolstoy gives us, but, while animated by Christ's spirit, by recognizing the changed conditions of this age, and adopting modes of expressing this spirit suitable to the changed conditions under which we live; still laboring for the good of our fellows, which was the essence of his life and teaching, but laboring in a different manner.

This, then, is held to be the duty of the man of Wealth: First, to set an example of modest, unostentatious living, shunning display or extravagance; to provide moderately for the legitimate wants of those dependent upon him; and after doing so to consider all surplus revenues which come to him simply as trust funds, which he is called upon to administer, and strictly bound as a matter of duty to administer in the manner which, in his judgment, is best calculated to produce the most beneficial results for the community—the man of wealth thus becoming the mere agent and trustee for his poorer brethren, bringing to their service his superior wisdom, experience and ability to administer, doing for them better than they would or could do for themselves.

We are met here with the difficulty of determining what are moderate sums to leave to members of the family; what is modest, unostentatious living; what is the test of extravagance. There must be different standards for different conditions. The answer is that it is as impossible to name exact amounts or actions as it is to define good manners, good taste, or the rules of propriety; but, nevertheless, these are verities, well known although undefinable. Public sentiment is quick to know and to feel what offends these. So in the case of wealth. The rule in regard to good taste in the dress of men or women applies here. Whatever makes one conspicuous offends the canon. If any family be chiefly known for display, for extravagance in home, table, equipage, for enormous sums ostentatiously spent in any form upon itself, if these be its chief distinctions, we have no difficulty in estimating its nature or culture. So likewise in regard to the use or abuse of its surplus wealth, or to generous, freehanded cooperation in good public uses, or to unabated efforts to accumulate and hoard to the last, whether they administer or bequeath. The verdict rests with the best and most enlightened public sentiment. The community will surely judge and its judgments will not often be wrong.

The best uses to which surplus wealth can be put have already been indicated. These who, would administer wisely must, indeed, be wise, for one of the serious obstacles to the improvement of our race is indiscriminate charity. It were better for mankind that the millions of the rich were thrown in to the sea than so spent as to encourage the slothful, the drunken, the unworthy. Of every thousand dollars spent in so called charity to-day, it is probable that $950 is unwisely spent; so spent, indeed as to produce the very evils which it proposes to mitigate or cure. A well-known writer of philosophic books admitted the other day that he had given a quarter of a dollar to a man who approached him as he was coming to visit the house of his friend. He knew nothing of the habits of this beggar; knew not the use that would be made of this money, although he had every reason to suspect that it would be spent improperly. This man professed to be a disciple of Herbert Spencer; yet the quarter-dollar given that night will probably work more injury than all the money which its thoughtless donor will ever be able to give in true charity will do good. He only gratified his own feelings, saved himself from annoyance, and this was probably one of the most selfish and very worst actions of his life, for in all respects he is most worthy.

In bestowing charity, the main consideration should be to help those who will help themselves; to provide part of the means by which those who desire to improve may do so; to give those who desire to use the aids by which they may rise; to assist, but rarely or never to do all. Neither the individual nor the race is improved by alms-giving. Those worthy of assistance, except in rare cases, seldom require assistance. The really valuable men of the race never do, except in cases of accident or sudden change. Every one has, of course, cases of individuals brought to his own knowledge where temporary assistance can do genuine good, and these he will not overlook. But the amount which can be wisely given by the individual for individuals is necessarily limited by his lack of knowledge of the circumstances connected with each. He is the only true reformer who is as careful and as anxious not to aid the unworthy as he is to aid the worthy, and, perhaps, even more so, for in alms-giving more injury is probably done by rewarding vice than by relieving virtue.

The rich man is thus almost restricted to following the examples of Peter Cooper, Enoch Pratt of Baltimore, Mr. Pratt of Brooklyn, Senator Stanford, and others, who know that the best means of benefiting the community is to place within its reach the ladders upon which the aspiring can rise–parks, and means of recreation, by which men are helped in body and mind; works of art, certain to give pleasure and improve the public taste, and public institutions of various kinds, which will improve the general condition of the people;–in this manner returning their surplus wealth to the mass of their fellows in the forms best calculated to do them lasting good.

Thus is the problem of Rich and Poor to be solved. The laws of accumulation will be left free; the laws of distribution free. Individualism will continue, but the millionaire will be but a trustee for the poor; entrusted for a season with a great part of the increased wealth of the community, but administering it for the community far better than it could or would have done for itself. The best minds will thus have reached a stage in the development of the race in which it is clearly seen that there is no mode of disposing of surplus wealth creditable to thoughtful and earnest men into whose hands it flows save by using it year by year for the general good. This day already dawns. But a little while, and although, without incurring the pity of their fellows, men may die sharers in great business enterprises from which their capital cannot be or has not been withdrawn, and is left chiefly at death for public uses, yet the man who dies leaving behind many millions of available wealth, which was his to administer during life, will pass away "unwept, unhonored, and unsung," no matter to what uses he leaves the dross which he cannot take with him. Of such as these the public verdict will then be : "The man who dies thus rich dies disgraced."

Such, in my opinion, is the true Gospel concerning Wealth, obedience to which is destined some day to solve the problem of the Rich and the Poor, and to bring "Peace on earth, among men Good-Will."

THE ECONOMIC POSSIBILITIES FOR OUR GRANDCHILDREN
John Maynard Keynes, 1930 (Public Domain)

We are suffering just now from a bad attack of economic pessimism. It is common to hear people say that the epoch of enormous economic progress which characterised the nineteenth century is over; that the rapid improvement in the standard of life is now going to slow down—at any rate in Great Britain; that a decline in prosperity is more likely than an improvement in the decade which lies ahead of us.

I believe that this is a wildly mistaken interpretation of what is happening to us. We are suffering, not from the rheumatics of old age, but from the growing-pains of over-rapid changes, from the painfulness of readjustment between one economic period and another. The increase of technical efficiency has been taking place faster than we can deal with the problem of labour absorption; the improvement in the standard of life has been a little too quick; the banking and monetary system of the world has been preventing the rate of interest from falling as fast as equilibrium requires. And even so, the waste and confusion which ensue relate to not more than 7½ per cent of the national income; we are muddling away one and sixpence in the £, and have only 18s. 6d., when we might, if we were more sensible, have £1; yet, nevertheless, the 18s. 6d. mounts up to as much as the £1 would have been five or six years ago. We forget that in 1929 the physical output of the industry of Great Britain was greater than ever before, and that the net surplus of our foreign balance available for new foreign investment, after paying for all our imports, was greater last year than that of any other country, being indeed 50 per cent greater than the corresponding surplus of the United States. Or again—if it is to be a matter of comparisons—suppose that we were to reduce our wages by a half, repudiate four-fifths of the national debt, and hoard our surplus wealth in barren gold instead of lending it at 6 per cent or more, we should resemble the now much-envied France. But would it be an improvement?

The prevailing world depression, the enormous anomaly of unemployment in a world full of wants, the disastrous mistakes we have made, blind us to what is going on under the surface—to the true interpretation of the trend of things. For I predict that both of the two opposed errors of pessimism which now make so much noise in the world will be proved wrong in our own time—the pessimism of the revolutionaries who think that things are so bad that nothing can save us but violent change, and the pessimism of the reactionaries who consider the balance of our economic and social life so precarious that we must risk no experiments.

My purpose in this essay, however, is not to examine the present or the near future, but to disembarrass myself of short views and take wings into the future. What can we reasonably the level of our economic life to be a hundred years hence? What are the economic possibilities for our grandchildren?

From the earliest times of which we have record—back, say, to two thousand years before Christ—down to the beginning of the eighteenth century, there was no very great change in the standard of life of the average man living in the civilised centres of the earth. Ups and downs certainly. Visitations of plague, famine, and war. Golden intervals. But no progressive, violent change. Some periods perhaps 50 per cent better than others—at the utmost 100 per cent better—in the four thousand years which ended (say) in A.D. 1700.

This slow rate of progress, or lack of progress, was due to two reasons—to the remarkable absence of important technical improvements and to the failure of capital to accumulate.

The absence of important technical inventions between the prehistoric age and comparatively modern times is truly remarkable. Almost everything which really matters and which the world possessed at the commencement of the modern age was already known to man at the dawn of history. Language, fire, the same domestic animals which we have to-day, wheat, barley, the vine and the olive, the plough, the wheel, the oar, the sail, leather, linen and cloth, bricks and pots, gold and silver, copper, tin, and lead—and iron was added to the list before 1000 B.C.—banking, statecraft, mathematics, astronomy, and religion. There is no record of when we first possessed these things.

At some epoch before the dawn of history—perhaps even in one of the comfortable intervals before the last ice age—there must have been an era of progress and invention comparable to that in which we live to-day. But through the greater part of recorded history there was nothing of the kind.

The modern age opened, I think, with the accumulation of capital which began in the sixteenth century. I believe—for reasons with which I must not encumber the present argument—that this was initially due to the rise of prices, and the profits to which that led, which resulted from the treasure of gold and silver which Spain brought from the New World into the Old. From that time until to-day the power of accumulation by compound interest, which seems to have been sleeping for many generations, was re-born and renewed its strength. And the power of compound interest over two hundred years is such as to stagger the imagination.

Let me give in illustration of this a sum which I have worked out. The value of Great Britain's foreign investments to-day is estimated at about £4,000,000,000. This yields us an income at the rate of about $6\frac{1}{2}$ per cent. Half of this we bring home and enjoy; the other half, namely, $3\frac{1}{4}$ per cent, we leave to accumulate abroad at compound interest. Something of this sort has now been going on for about 250 years.

For I trace the beginnings of British foreign investment to the treasure which Drake stole from Spain in 1580. In that year he returned to England bringing with him the prodigious spoils of the Golden Hind. Queen Elizabeth was a considerable shareholder in the syndicate which had financed the expedition. Out of her share she paid off the whole of England's foreign debt, balanced her Budget, and found herself with about £40,000 in hand. This she invested in the Levant Company—which prospered. Out of the profits of the Levant Company, the East India Company was founded; and the profits of this great enterprise were the foundation of England's subsequent foreign investment. Now it happens that £40,000 accumulating at 3¼ per cent compound interest approximately corresponds to the actual volume of England's foreign investments at various dates, and would actually amount to-day to the total of £4,000,000,000 which I have already quoted as being what our foreign investments now are. Thus, every £1 which Drake brought home in 1580 has now become £100,000. Such is the power of compound interest!

From the sixteenth century, with a cumulative crescendo after the eighteenth, the great age of science and technical inventions began, which since the beginning of the nineteenth century has been in full flood—coal, steam, electricity, petrol, steel, rubber, cotton, the chemical industries, automatic machinery and the methods of mass production, wireless, printing, Newton, Darwin, and Einstein, and thousands of other things and men too famous and familiar to catalogue.

What is the result? In spite of an enormous growth in the population of the world, which it has been necessary to equip with houses and machines, the average standard of life in Europe and the United States has been raised, I think, about fourfold. The growth of capital has been on a scale which is far beyond a hundred-fold of what any previous age had known. And from now on we need not expect so great an increase of population.

If capital increases, say, 2 per cent per annum, the capital equipment of the world will have increased by a half in twenty years, and seven and a half times in a hundred years. Think of this in terms of material things—houses, transport, and the like.

At the same time technical improvements in manufacture and transport have been proceeding at a greater rate in the last ten years than ever before in history. In the United States factory output per head was 40 per cent greater in 1925 than in 1919. In Europe we are held back by temporary obstacles, but even so it is safe to say that technical efficiency is increasing by more than 1 per cent per annum compound. There is evidence that the revolutionary technical changes, which have so far chiefly affected industry, may soon be attacking agriculture. We may be on the eve of improvements in the efficiency of food production as great as those which have already taken place in mining, manufacture, and transport. In quite a few years—in our own lifetimes I mean—we may be able to perform all the operations of agriculture, mining, and manufacture with a quarter of the human effort to which we have been accustomed.

For the moment the very rapidity of these changes is hurting us and bringing difficult problems to solve. Those countries are suffering relatively which are not in the vanguard of progress. We are being afflicted with a new disease of which some readers may not yet have heard the name, but of which they will hear a great deal in the years to come—namely, technological unemployment. This means unemployment due to our discovery of means of economising the use of labour outrunning the pace at which we can find new uses for labour.

But this is only a temporary phase of maladjustment. All this means in the long run that mankind is solving its economic problem. I would predict that the standard of life in progressive countries one hundred years hence will be between four and eight times as high as it is to-day. There would be nothing surprising in this even in the light of our present knowledge. It would not be foolish to contemplate the possibility of a far greater progress still.

Let us, for the sake of argument, suppose that a hundred years hence we are all of us, on the average, eight times better off in the economic sense than we are to-day. Assuredly there need be nothing here to surprise us.

Now it is true that the needs of human beings may seem to be insatiable. But they fall into two classes—those needs which are absolute in the sense that we feel them whatever the situation of our fellow human beings may be, and those which are relative in the sense that we feel them only if their satisfaction lifts us above, makes us feel superior to, our fellows. Needs of the second class, those which satisfy the desire for superiority, may indeed be insatiable; for the higher the general level, the higher still are they. But this is not so true of the absolute needs—a point may soon be reached, much sooner perhaps than we are all of us aware of, when these needs are satisfied in the sense that we prefer to devote our further energies to non-economic purposes.

Now for my conclusion, which you will find, I think, to become more and more startling to the imagination the longer you think about it.

I draw the conclusion that, assuming no important wars and no important increase in population, the economic problem may be solved, or be at least within sight of solution, within a hundred years. This means that the economic problem is not—if we look into the future—the permanent problem of the human race.

Why, you may ask, is this so startling? It is startling because—if, instead of looking into the future, we look into the past—we find that the economic problem, the struggle for subsistence, always has been hitherto the primary, most pressing problem of the human race—not only of the human race, but of the whole of the biological kingdom from the beginnings of life in its most primitive forms.

Thus we have been expressly evolved by nature—with all

our impulses and deepest instincts—for the purpose of solving the economic problem. If the economic problem is solved, mankind will be deprived of its traditional purpose.

Will this be a benefit? If one believes at all in the real values of life, the prospect at least opens up the possibility of benefit. Yet I think with dread of the readjustment of the habits and instincts of the ordinary man, bred into him for countless generations, which he may be asked to discard within a few decades.

To use the language of to-day—must we not expect a general "nervous breakdown"? We already have a little experience of what I mean—a nervous breakdown of the sort which is already common enough in England and the United States amongst the wives of the well-to-do classes, unfortunate women, many of them, who have been deprived by their wealth of their traditional tasks and occupations—who cannot find it sufficiently amusing, when deprived of the spur of economic necessity, to cook and clean and mend, yet are quite unable to find anything more amusing.

To those who sweat for their daily bread leisure is a longed-for sweet—until they get it.

There is the traditional epitaph written for herself by the old charwoman:—

Don't mourn for me, friends, don't weep for me never,
For I'm going to do nothing for ever and ever.

This was her heaven. Like others who look forward to leisure, she conceived how nice it would be to spend her time listening-in—for there was another couplet which occurred in her poem:—

With psalms and sweet music the heavens'll be ringing,
But I shall have nothing to do with the singing.

Yet it will only be for those who have to do with the singing that life will be tolerable—and how few of us can sing!

Thus for the first time since his creation man will be faced with his real, his permanent problem—how to use his freedom

JOHN MAYNARD KEYNES

from pressing economic cares, how to occupy the leisure, which science and compound interest will have won for him, to live wisely and agreeably and well.

The strenuous purposeful money-makers may carry all of us along with them into the lap of economic abundance. But it will be those peoples, who can keep alive, and cultivate into a fuller perfection, the art of life itself and do not sell themselves for the means of life, who will be able to enjoy the abundance when it comes.

Yet there is no country and no people, I think, who can look forward to the age of leisure and of abundance without a dread. For we have been trained too long to strive and not to enjoy. It is a fearful problem for the ordinary person, with no special talents, to occupy himself, especially if he no longer has roots in the soil or in custom or in the beloved conventions of a traditional society. To judge from the behaviour and the achievements of the wealthy classes to-day in any quarter of the world, the outlook is very depressing! For these are, so to speak, our advance guard—those who are spying out the promised land for the rest of us and pitching their camp there. For they have most of them failed disastrously, so it seems to me—those who have an independent income but no associations or duties or ties—to solve the problem which has been set them.

I feel sure that with a little more experience we shall use the new-found bounty of nature quite differently from the way in which the rich use it to-day, and will map out for ourselves a plan of life quite otherwise than theirs.

For many ages to come the old Adam will be so strong in us that everybody will need to do some work if he is to be contented. We shall do more things for ourselves than is usual with the rich to-day, only too glad to have small duties and tasks and routines. But beyond this, we shall endeavour to spread the bread thin on the butter—to make what work there is still to be done to be as widely shared as possible. Three-hour shifts or a fifteen-hour week may put off the problem for a great while. For three hours a day is quite enough to satisfy the old Adam in most of us!

There are changes in other spheres too which we must expect to come. When the accumulation of wealth is no longer of high social importance, there will be great changes in the code of morals. We shall be able to rid ourselves of many of the pseudo-moral principles which have hag-ridden us for two hundred years, by which we have exalted some of the most distasteful of human qualities into the position of the highest virtues. We shall be able to afford to dare to assess the money-motive at its true value. The love of money as a possession—as distinguished from the love of money as a means to the enjoyments and realities of life—will be recognised for what it is, a somewhat disgusting morbidity, one of those semi-criminal, semi-pathological propensities which one hands over with a shudder to the specialists in mental disease. All kinds of social customs and economic practices, affecting the distribution of wealth and of economic rewards and penalties, which we now maintain at all costs, however distasteful and unjust they may be in themselves, because they are tremendously useful in promoting the accumulation of capital, we shall then be free, at last, to discard.

Of course there will still be many people with intense, unsatisfied purposiveness who will blindly pursue wealth—unless they can find some plausible substitute. But the rest of us will no longer be under any obligation to applaud and encourage them. For we shall inquire more curiously than is safe to-day into the true character of this "purposiveness" with which in varying degrees Nature has endowed almost all of us. For purposiveness means that we are more concerned with the remote future results of our actions than with their own quality or their immediate effects on our own environment. The "purposive" man is always trying to secure a spurious and delusive immortality for his acts by pushing his interest in them forward into time. He does not love his cat, but his cat's kittens; nor, in truth, the kittens, but only the kittens' kittens, and so on forward for ever to the end of cat-dom. For him jam is not jam unless it is a case of jam to-morrow and never jam to-day. Thus by pushing his jam always forward into the future, he strives to secure for his act of boiling it an immortality.

Let me remind you of the Professor in Sylvie and Bruno:—

"Only the tailor, sir, with your little bill," said a meek voice outside the door.

"Ah, well, I can soon settle his business," the Professor said to the children, "if you'll just wait a minute. How much is it, this year, my man?" The tailor had come in while he was speaking.

"Well, it's been a-doubling so many years, you see," the tailor replied, a little gruffly, "and I think I'd like the money now. It's two thousand pound, it is!"

"Oh, that's nothing!" the Professor carelessly remarked, feeling in his pocket, as if he always carried at least that amount about with him. "But wouldn't you like to wait just another year and make it four thousand? Just think how rich you'd be! Why, you might be a king, if you liked!"

"I don't know as I'd care about being a king," the man said thoughtfully. "But it dew sound a powerful sight o' money! Well, I think I'll wait."

"Of course you will!" said the Professor. "There's good sense in you, I see. Good-day to you, my man!"

"Will you ever have to pay him that four thousand pounds?" Sylvie asked as the door closed on the departing creditor.

"Never, my child!" the Professor replied emphatically. "He'll go on doubling it till he dies. You see, it's always worth while waiting another year to get twice as much money!"

Perhaps it is not an accident that the race which did most to bring the promise of immortality into the heart and essence of our religions has also done most for the principle of compound interest and particularly loves this most purposive of human institutions.

I see us free, therefore, to return to some of the most sure and certain principles of religion and traditional virtue—that avarice is a vice, that the exaction of usury is a misdemeanour, and the love of money is detestable, that those walk most truly in the paths of virtue and sane wisdom who take least thought for the morrow. We shall once more value ends above means and prefer the good to the useful. We shall honour those who can teach us how to pluck the hour and the day virtuously and well, the delightful people who are capable of taking direct enjoyment in things, the lilies of the field who toil not, neither do they spin.

But beware! The time for all this is not yet. For at least another hundred years we must pretend to ourselves and to every one that fair is foul and foul is fair; for foul is useful and fair is not. Avarice and usury and precaution must be our gods for a little longer still. For only they can lead us out of the tunnel of economic necessity into daylight.

I look forward, therefore, in days not so very remote, to the greatest change which has ever occurred in the material environment of life for human beings in the aggregate. But, of course, it will all happen gradually, not as a catastrophe. Indeed, it has already begun. The course of affairs will simply be that there will be ever larger and larger classes and groups of people from whom problems of economic necessity have been practically removed. The critical difference will be realised when this condition has become so general that the nature of one's duty to one's neighbour is changed. For it will remain reasonable to be economically purposive for others after it has ceased to be reasonable for oneself.

JOHN MAYNARD KEYNES

The pace at which we can reach our destination of economic bliss will be governed by four things—our power to control population, our determination to avoid wars and civil dissensions, our willingness to entrust to science the direction of those matters which are properly the concern of science, and the rate of accumulation as fixed by the margin between our production and our consumption; of which the last will easily look after itself, given the first three.

Meanwhile there will be no harm in making mild preparations for our destiny, in encouraging, and experimenting in, the arts of life as well as the activities of purpose.

But, chiefly, do not let us overestimate the importance of the economic problem, or sacrifice to its supposed necessities other matters of greater and more permanent significance. It should be a matter for specialists—like dentistry. If economists could manage to get themselves thought of as humble, competent people, on a level with dentists, that would be splendid!

CORPORATE EMPATHY
Vinny Tafuro

September 2012

CONTENTS

Introduction   77

Prologue   78
Innovation and Automation
A Brief History of the United States
Launching the Technical Revolution
Section I: Visions Lost   86
Thoughts on the Present State of World Affairs
Experimental Prototype Community Of Tomorrow (EPCOT)
Corporate Consolidation and Shareholder Fiduciary Duty
Reaching the Lowest Common Denominator
The Wizard of OZ and Frankenstein
Section II: Embracing a Revolution   97
Redefining Public
Enter Women
Connecting Dots and Changing the World
Education
Generation Empathy
Section III: Instilling Empathy   110
Moore's Law
A Psychological Evaluation of Corporations
Finding Purpose
Betray the Age

INTRODUCTION

Empathy: The ability to understand and share the feelings of another.

Empathy is a powerful human emotion. It is the reason we have advanced as a civilization. It is this emotion, combined with America's adoption of capitalism through the American Revolution, that allowed our country's greatest inventors and innovators to improve our world in profound ways.

Thanks to their innovation and the economies of scale of our corporations, we have been able to nurture technology and harness our natural resources bringing us to where we are today.

Our best chance to fully embrace innovation and technology and move humanity forward is to empower corporations to utilize the human emotion of empathy.

Perhaps the sentiments contained in the following pages, are not yet sufficiently fashionable to procure them general favor; a long habit of not thinking a thing wrong, gives it a superficial appearance of being right, and raises at first a formidable outcry in defence of custom. But the tumult soon subsides. Time makes more converts than reason.
– Thomas Paine, *Common Sense*

In the following pages I will review how America and our world's corporations have come to our current place, define through examples where this system is flawed, and finally lay out ideas for solving the deficiencies in the system.

VINNY TAFURO

PROLOGUE

Innovation and Automation

America's establishment of an independent republic by the people for the people, for the first time in history, transferred the methods of production and benefits of capitalism from a select few to the masses. The proliferation of its accessibility has been challenging as it has expanded over the past two and half centuries in step with our own human evolution and expectation of civil rights and equality. We've come a long way from child and slave labor and the unequal rights of women.

As technology and our economy evolved through the industrial age, we have been able to influence its development through government regulation; union and trade association strikes and policy; and consumer actions such as boycotts and consumer review.

The dawn of personal computing and proliferation of the Internet ushered in the technological revolution and marked the end of the American industrial age. The subsequent outsourcing of our low-wage industrial jobs is being mistaken as a slide in American innovation instead of being seen for the opportunity that it is.

Automation and technology free people to learn and innovate more. Each job that our country is able to outsource effectively has two benefits that are not currently well recognized or utilized. Each outsourced job allows a foreign citizen to grow economically, while at the same time freeing more of our own population to invest more time in education and subsequently increase opportunities to innovate.

When Google Chairman Eric Schmidt spoke at a forum jointly hosted by Google and the Pittsburgh Technology Council on September 23, 2009, in Pittsburgh, he compared the development of the mechanical loom to our current economic situation.

If you look at the history of—a typical example would be the loom, in 1860, 1870 if I get my dates right. The development of the mechanical loom ultimately was one of the key components of the rise of the Industrial Revolution that ultimately built things like Pittsburg and so forth and so on.

When they study what happened with the loom, it displaced a very large number of people who were previously doing it by hand. The bad news for those people was that they did not get new high paying jobs. Their children did.

So the real problem with all the changes that I'm talking about is a generational one. I'm very confident that an innovation agenda around advanced manufacturing and the things America does well will replace the jobs that we've lost, for example, high-volume, low-tech manufacturing, but the jobs will be numeric jobs. They will be the children of the people who lost the jobs. The people who lost the jobs will probably not come back and that's a real tragedy for them.

Our current workforce is experiencing a similar period to those who were displaced by the mechanical loom. The Internet has fundamentally changed how the world communicates, learns and does business. The loom laid the foundation for the Industrial Revolution; personal computing and the Internet are the catalysts of the Technological Revolution.

While we are now firmly in the technology age, we are not in control of its development. The entities that guided corporations during the Industrial Revolution are not properly suited to do the same moving forward. Technology is developing so quickly that government regulation, industry policy, and union and consumer action are no longer effective in keeping industries from purposely, or even accidentally, harming the public good.

Modern technology companies Apple, Google and Facebook illustrate a dynamic shift between the two ages. The founders of all three companies were focused on creating social change first, with profitability being secondary at best.

Most recently, Mark Zuckerberg's statements on corporate governance and the mission of Facebook in the company's IPO Registration Statement prior to going public clearly define the values that will guide the company's decisions.

Facebook was not originally created to be a company. It was built to accomplish a social mission - to make the world more open and connected.

We think it's important that everyone who invests in Facebook understands what this mission means to us, how we make decisions and why we do the things we do.

The companies of the Industrial Revolution were created to establish change as well, albeit differently. The automation of production that began with inventions like the mechanical loom and printing press were fully realized with the maturity of the assembly line by Henry Ford and followed by robotic automation.

The manufacturing and production jobs lost to automation were replaced by service jobs. The service jobs and remaining manufacturing jobs that are being lost to technology and outsourcing will subsequently have to find a new replacement.

The millennial generation will be the first beneficiaries of the Technological Revolution. They are not lazy or unwilling to work; they are not soft; they are not unwilling to learn. The world view of this segment of the population can be summarized by a now-famous statement made by Steve Jobs during his Stanford University commencement address in 2005.

For the past 33 years, I have looked in the mirror every morning and asked myself, "If today was the last day of my life, would I want to do what I am about to do today?" And whenever the answer has been "No" for too many days in a row, I know I need to change something… Almost everything - all external expectations, all pride, all fear of embarrassment or failure - these things just fall away in the face of death, leaving only what is truly important. Remembering that you are going to die is the best way I know to avoid the trap of thinking you have something to lose.

Technology, automation and outsourcing are providing a means for a growing segment of the world's population to live by the above statement.

A Brief History of the United States

The progress made during the industrial revolution and throughout America's history has been messy and at times shameful. Pick any chapter in *A People's History of the United States* by Howard Zinn for plenty of examples. That said, the strength of the United States Constitution has allowed those who were at first treated harshly to eventually find equality.

It has been a hard journey, but along the way Americans who felt empathy for their fellow Americans have worked diligently to change things for the better.

Pre-Civil War America

The years following the Revolutionary War were marked by rapid territorial expansion and constant cultural clashes, combined with innovations that led to the American Industrial Revolution. The idea of American expansionism evolved into the concept of manifest destiny as we expanded our border west and added states to the union. Our Constitution allowed for the first time a population to govern itself, which led to civil rights and labor advances by forcing the American people to continuously re-evaluate how we treat others. Technical innovation such as the mechanical loom, sewing machine, telegraph and photography improved automation and communication.

The expansion of the United States brought with it a number of wars and skirmishes as we encountered and displaced Native Americans and forced conflicts with European and Mexican inhabitants. The War of 1812 and the

Mexican War were both instigated by the United States as we violently expanded our borders. Passage of The Indian Removal Act in 1830 illustrated our immature view of equality.

Innovations in technology allowed for mechanization and increased production of goods and services. The invention of the cotton gin by Eli Whitney and the first power loom by Edmund Cartwright in the late 18th century caused a rise in slavery in the South and unemployment in the North, increasing tensions between the two regions that would eventually lead to the Civil War.

The development of the telegraph and photography in the 1830s would enable instant communication and the transfer of visually impactful images over long distances for the first time. The human experience changed through increased communication and our ability to feel empathy for a larger community.

Industry Shapes America

An idealist is a person who helps other people to be prosperous.
– Henry Ford

As our country transitioned from the 19th to 20th century, the Industrial Revolution gained momentum and regularly began to test the limits of our recent gains in civil and human rights by pressing consumers and laborers with hard challenges. Many of our labor unions and consumer protection laws are rooted in struggles from this period of history.

It was also a time of great strides in technology and science. The telephone, Kodak camera, motion pictures and the automobile were all huge advances that increased communication among people. The telephone allowed instant verbal communication of ideas, and the Kodak camera brought the power of photography to the masses. The motion picture brought a new depth of reality to the visual image.

One of the most influential developments was the mass production of automobiles, credited to Henry Ford's implementation of the assembly line. With Ford's mass produced cars, Americans would have access to a simple transportation method that allowed them to freely explore the country further from home.

I will build a car for the great multitude. It will be large enough for the family, but small enough for the individual to run and care for. It will be constructed of the best materials, by the best men to be hired, after the simplest designs that modern engineering can devise. But it will be so low in price that no man making a good salary will be unable to own one — and enjoy with his family the blessing of hours of pleasure in God's great open spaces.

Ford was an idealist in that he created his vehicles first as a method of affordable quality transportation. Only because he was successful with the primary goal, was he also very profitable.

Ford's cars loaded with families holding Kodak cameras would create a wave of interaction, compassion and empathy across the country that can still be seen to this day in our love of the car and road trips

The Great Depression

The Great Depression illustrated America's true values of strength, survival and compassion fueled by empathy. Triggered by the crash of 1929, it was a period of dark despair for a country that had in just the previous decade been wildly celebrating what seemed like an endless bounty created by the Industrial Revolution.

A majority of Americans were willing to work but unable to find jobs. Those with something helped others possessing only a willingness to get to a better place.

While the Great Depression did not create many great advances in technology, it did create a generation of Americans who understood exactly how important life, liberty and the pursuit of happiness were to the world. This generation understood it so well that they would win a world war in the name of freedom from tyranny and become known as America's Greatest Generation.

A Changing World

The vast majority of innovation during the Industrial Revolution prior to WWII was grounded in our understanding of mechanics and simple observable scientific evidence. The massive wartime investment in science and technology pushed both fields into areas where experimentation and theory created new laws of science that would feed the development of exponentially growing technologies.

Baby Boom & Suburban Development

The prosperity and confidence that America experienced following WWII kicked off a baby boom and the beginning of suburban development with transit and the automobile, allowing us to live further from urban centers. Innovators like William Levitt applied Henrys Ford's production line concept to home building. This occurred across the country and included Levitt's suburban Long Island community of Levittown near my hometown of Westbury. The economies of scale created by production lines and market competition across all industries allowed large numbers of Americans to afford home ownership among other new and convenient amenities.

Launching the Technical Revolution

Until the 1970s, wide usage of computer technologies was limited to experimentation by governments, universities and corporations because the cost of access was high and the uses were beyond what any individual had a practical application for. However, during a period of social revolution, college dropouts Bill Gates and Steve Jobs, through simultaneous competition and collaboration, opened the gateway of the Technology Revolution to everyone.

The introduction of the personal computer and subsequent growth of communication created by the Internet would signal the closing doors on the industrial age and the coming struggle by America to embrace the new reality it was responsible for creating.

SECTION I: VISIONS LOST

Thoughts on the Present State of World Affairs

Post World War II America has been marked by constant social struggle as our society has learned to adapt to the exponential growth of communication and information brought on by technology. The wide proliferation of television followed by the personal computer and the Internet dramatically increased the amount and ease of communication between people all over the world.

In our lifetimes we're going from almost no one being able to communicate to almost everyone being able to communicate. We're also going from almost no one having any kind of information and access to libraries, to virtually everyone having access to every piece of information in the world. That is an enormous accomplishment for humanity.
– Eric Schmidt, Chairman of Google

In the following pages I will illustrate with factual references and simple urging how human empathy has not been embraced by our public corporations and how that lack of human emotion has severely limited the capabilities of our companies to truly innovate in the way their founders had envisioned.

I will decidedly avoid a number of subjects that are already well documented and debated and would otherwise diminish the purpose of this book. My goal is to provide the reader with enough information to provoke thought, encourage dialog and stimulate action.

Experimental Prototype Community Of Tomorrow (EPCOT)

Growing up on Long Island I lived only a couple of miles from Levittown, a planned community of mass produced homes developed between 1947 and 1951. The returning veterans of World War II fueled much of this growth as well as similar suburban growth throughout the country. The economies of scale that production lines created allowed large numbers of Americans to own a home.

William Levitt, the developer of Levittown, is an example of an innovator following Henry Ford's concept of providing a high quality product inexpensively to the masses in order to improve life. Ford, passionate about automation, experimented with city planning using technology. Walt Disney, a friend of Ford, shared these same qualities culminating with his vision for the Experimental Prototype Community Of Tomorrow, more commonly known as EPCOT to be built at Disney World in Florida.

EPCOT will take its cue from the new ideas and new technologies that are now emerging from the creative centers of American industry. It will be a community of tomorrow that will never be completed, that will always be introducing and testing and demonstrating new materials and new systems; and EPCOT will always be a showcase to the world for the ingenuity and imagination of American free enterprise. I don't believe there is a challenge anywhere in the world that's more important to people everywhere than finding solutions to the problems of our cities. – Walt Disney

Unlike the theme park that bears the name today, Disney's own view of EPCOT was that of an ever-evolving experimental community.

Well a project like this is so vast in scope that no one company alone can make it a reality. But if we can bring together the technical know-how of American industry and the creative imagination of the Disney organization, I'm confident we can create right here in Disney World a

showcase to the world of the American free enterprise system. I believe we can build a community that more people talk about and come to look at than any other area in the world, and with your cooperation I'm sure that this Experimental Prototype Community of Tomorrow can influence the future of city living for generations to come. It's an exciting challenge, a once in a lifetime opportunity for everyone who participates. Speaking for myself and the entire Disney organization, we're ready to go right now. – Walt Disney

Disney's vision of EPCOT was why Orlando and the state of Florida granted the company expansive rights over the property Disney owned. The plans to develop EPCOT would require Disney to make land use and building decisions free from politics allowing them to adapt and change more quickly. The agreement goes so far as to even allow the company to construct a nuclear power plant on the property if it desires.

Here the Disney staff will work with individual companies to create a showcase of industry at work. In attractive park-like settings, the 6 million people who visit Disney World each year will look behind the scenes at experimental prototype plants, research and development laboratories, and computer centers for major corporations.

So this is EPCOT, the heart of Disney World. In other parts of the country, a community the size of this prototype could become part of an entire city complex, composed of many such communities, planned and built a few miles apart. In Disney World about 20 thousand people will live in EPCOT. Their homes will be built in ways that permit ease of change so that new products may continuously be demonstrated. Their schools will welcome new ideas so that everyone who grows up in EPCOT will have skills in pace with today's world. EPCOT will be a working community with employment for all; and everyone who lives here will have a responsibility to help keep this community an exciting living blueprint of the future. – Disney World Promotional Video

Five months after Walt Disney's death in December 1966, Florida Governor Claude R. Kirk, Jr. signed into Florida law the statutes creating the Reedy Creek Improvement District that gave the Disney organization almost total autonomy within its borders. However, with Walt gone, the publicly traded Walt Disney Company had lost its founder and his unique ability to innovate and inspire. His brother Roy O. Disney tried to carry the EPCOT project forward but was unable to convince Disney's board of directors to do so.

Empathy Lost

The most exciting, by far the most important part of our Florida project, in fact the heart of everything we'll be doing in Disney World, will be our Experimental Prototype City of Tomorrow. We call it EPCOT. – Walt Disney

Despite Walt considering EPCOT as the heart of everything the company would be doing in Florida and the expansive rights (and responsibilities) given to the company by the government, the Disney board would not pursue the project. Walt's EPCOT project was diluted down to a theme park opened in 1982 and known mostly for food and drinks from around the world in the park's internationally-themed World Showcase.

Under the later direction of CEO Michael Eisner, the company launched into heavy hotel and resort development on the property, placing strains on the communities of Orlando and Orange and Osceola counties. Using its expansive rights in a very non-empathetic way, the board of directors saw no problem competing for and winning government bond money for its own expansion. Disney won the money to pay for its own new sewers rather than it being spent on an affordable housing project needed by the county for the influx of low-wage Disney workers.

Walt Disney World's governmental arm is a real city in the eyes of the Florida Constitution and has the right to compete with other governments for tax-exempt bonds, an Orange County judge has ruled.

In dismissing a lawsuit filed by Republican candidate for governor Anthony R. Martin, Circuit Judge George N. Diamantis said the Reedy

Creek Improvement District acted within the law when it applied for and received $57 million in tax-exempt bonds that Orange County had hoped to use to build affordable housing. – Orlando Sentinel, 1990

The rights granted to the company because of its founder's visionary ideas had been executed by a board and company that do not share his vision. In 1997 BusinessWeek named Disney's board the worst board of directors in American business. By the time Eisner was pushed out as CEO in 2005. Walt's own nephew Roy E. Disney had written "that the Company is rapacious, soul-less, and always looking for the 'quick buck' rather than the long-term value, which is leading to a loss of public trust."

The American Dream and suburban development was in its infancy following WWII. Had Disney's innovative EPCOT project been implemented and even mildly successful, its effect on the subsequent decades of suburban development would have been nothing short of profound.

Innovation Lost

While abandoning EPCOT was a huge loss to society, it is this loss of a founder's vision fueled by empathy that is at the root of many of our struggles with corporate America today. There are countless examples of companies that make decisions which are not in line with the founder's values, as well as times when companies simply oust the founder directly for not being profit-motivated enough.

Many of the corporations of today were founded by individuals whose primary goal was to provide a product or service to customers better than anyone else currently doing so; feeding the family was important, but so was treating your customers and employees well.

When a company goes public, the founder typically loses a great deal of control to keep their personal values and subsequent innovation and vision incorporated into the business. The longer the company exists and the further removed the founder, the more diluted the company's values become.

The aging company no longer has the vision and empathy of the founder, leaving behind a new CEO and board of directors that are only able to keep the company as innovative as shareholders will allow. The company begins to make more and more decisions based on profits and less on the vision of the founder.

Corporate Consolidation and Shareholder Fiduciary Duty

The natural tendency of corporations to consolidate and expand is a progression of capitalism fueled by the benefits of economies of scale that are realized by larger systems over smaller ones. The family farm has been replaced by the corporate farm, the general store by big box retail, and mutual aid societies have been replaced by the insurance, media and entertainment industries to name only a few.

Exponential growth of science and technology has magnified the benefits of larger economies of scale while our methods of regulation have struggled to keep up.

Jet Blue

Jet Blue has run advertisements promising "to continue to bring humanity back to air travel," and the company states that they exist "to provide superior service in every aspect of our customer's air travel experience." While JetBlue's founder and former CEO David Neeleman may have started the company with the above as a first priority, he was unable to maintain it.

He was ousted as CEO just three months after apologizing on national TV for the service problems the company experienced during a big winter storm in 2007 that left hundreds of passengers stranded on planes for hours.

Author Simon Sinek, in a 2008 blog post, *The Battered-Wife Customer Service Model*, said that "with or without Neeleman at the helm, honesty and humanity should still prevail at JetBlue…" and closed commenting, "I'm just sad to see one of the few companies who believed in customer [service] first start to show signs of cracking."

It is unlikely under current conditions that the company will improve service or do any better. JetBlue's customer service and priorities will likely continue to degrade until they reach an acceptable lowest common denominator of service equal to other airlines. To attempt anything better would be seen as a failure to maximize profits.

Edison General Electric Company (GE)

I never perfected an invention that I did not think about in terms of the service it might give others... I find out what the world needs, then I proceed to invent... – Thomas Edison

Thomas Edison, founder of Edison General Electric Company (today known as GE), is one of the most prolific innovators and inventors in history, holding over 1,000 US patents alone, along with many others in the United Kingdom, France and Germany. He is credited with numerous inventions that contributed to mass communication and most famously the first commercially viable light bulb.

The year was 1876, America's centennial, and for most Americans, a time for looking backward with pride. For others like Thomas Edison it was a time to look forward to the possibilities that lay ahead. The electrical exhibits at the Centennial Exposition in Philadelphia marked the beginning of a productive new era of harnessing our imagination.

1876 was also the year that Thomas Alva Edison opened a laboratory in Menlo Park, New Jersey, where he could explore the possibilities of the dynamo and other electrical devices that he had seen in

the Exposition. Out of that laboratory was to come perhaps the greatest invention of the age - a successful incandescent electric lamp. – GE website

During a segment of 60 Minutes in October 2011, Barbara Walters interviewed General Electric's current Chairman Jeffrey Immelt who had recently been named President Barack Obama's Jobs Czar. Immelt's answer below about whether companies have a civic responsibility to create jobs is likely different than what Edison might have said.

My name is not above the door. I work for investors. Investors want to see us grow earnings and cash flow. They want to see us be competitive and prosper… I want you to say, win GE. I think this notion that it's the population of the US against the big companies; it's just wrong-minded. … our employees basically like us… They root for us. They want us to win. I don't know why you don't.

The statement above speaks nothing of innovation, only of winning, but winning what? While the company is still innovating, GE will only take financial risks that are likely to be profitable within a single quarter or year or two. To look beyond that would be considered too risky for investors.

Wal-Mart

Outstanding leaders go out of their way to boost the self-esteem of their personnel. If people believe in themselves, it's amazing what they can accomplish. – Sam Walton

Sam and Helen Walton opened the first Walton's 5-10 in 1950, a Ben Franklin franchise, which the Walton family expanded to nine stores by 1959. In 1962 Sam opened his first large discount store under the WALMART name in Rogers, Arkansas, which led him to his innovative idea of opening discount stores in rural areas, which were currently underserved communities.

In the early years a driving value behind Wal-Mart's growth

would be a constant desire to continually improve efficiency and become a better company. In 1972 when Wal-Mart went public, Sam and Helen Walton made sure their 3,500 employees were made associates through a generous profit-sharing program.

Since its founding through the 1980s, Wal-Mart enjoyed a relatively good public image and seemed to hold many of Sam Walton's values along the way. It was not until after Sam's death that leadership in the company became diluted by leadership that did not share Sam's empathy and desire to keep improving.

Sam Walton set the standard for listening to his customers and listening to the people who do the work. In addition to being a great entrepreneur and business leader, Sam Walton was, above all, a fine, decent, kind, generous man. I will miss him. We all will miss him.
– H. Ross Perot

In 2010 CEO Mike Duke, after being at the helm since only 2009, ended the profit-sharing program that Sam Walton had created in an effort to increase profitability.

Today, along with a CEO facing allegations of corruption and bribery, Walmart's general business practices can no longer be described as following the values of the empathetic person that Sam Walton was.

Reaching the Lowest Common Denominator

The industrial age rewarded diverse competition as inventors and entrepreneurs raced to create the next new innovation. In the technology age, innovation often requires a winner-take-all approach with multiple companies creating products that operate on a standardized system. Think of VHS, DVD and Blu-Ray as examples of the progression of standardization.

Companies that have lost their founder's empathy and

innovative drive typically produce lower quality products in the name of increasing profits. This subsequently also creates a race to the bottom in whichever industry it occurs.

Apple vs. Microsoft

The battle between Steve Jobs' Apple and Bill Gates' Microsoft for the personal computer market is the perfect example of how this can work in the technological age. When Apple released the Apple II in 1977, the computer was immediately popular and the company grew exponentially, leading it to go public in 1980. Once public, Apple was no longer controlled solely by Jobs who by 1985 was ousted as CEO by the board of directors.

Between 1985 and Jobs' eventual return to Apple in 1996, the personal computer market become flooded with products by companies trying to replicate Apple's initial success. These competing products only succeeded in commoditizing PCs into a price war, which was eventually won by Microsoft where Gates had provided the Windows operating system to be run on a wide variety of hardware.

With the innovative ideas and intuitive vision of Jobs no longer at Apple, the company made decisions based on profits and market trends that lead Apple down the same path as the rest of the industry. It was not until Jobs' return to Apple that the company began its climb back to relevance in the PC market, as well as dominance in industries that had previously not involved computers or simply never existed before.

The Wizard of OZ & Frankenstein

The story of the Wizard of OZ was written over 100 years ago as an allegory of the fight for power over money between people and American industry, which were portrayed by the Cowardly Lion, Scarecrow and Tin Man, and the Wall Street and Chicago Banks portrayed by the Wicked Witches of the East and West.

The story only described the symptoms; the money supply was limited and the banks were evil. The story did not address why the banks were evil. Like today we debate whether large companies are evil. They are not evil. They are just not structured to make truly empathetic decisions.

To illustrate the actual cause for corporations acting seemingly evil, the story of Frankenstein does a much better job at defining the cause. Frankenstein's creation was given life but lacked a soul and empathy. It learned a sense of compassion. It sought acceptance. It even understood it was ugly.

Capitalism is our adopted child. We currently benefit greatly from the technology it produces but are subservient to its whims. We must empower our child with the ability to be accepted and grow responsibly on its own.

The monster concludes its story with a demand that Frankenstein create for it a female companion like itself. It argues that as a living thing, it has a right to happiness and that Victor, as its creator, has a duty to obey it, with the chilling words, "You are my creator, but I am your master. Obey!" – *Wikipedia*, July 2012

Today we are still in control of our capitalistic economy and the technology it produces; however, our corporations act with a seemingly sociopathic indifference towards the very consumers that they serve. It is in this time that we must encourage our public companies to act in the same empathetic manner we expect of ourselves as individuals.

SECTION II: EMBRACING A REVOLUTION

Throughout the previous pages I have explored the path that America has taken to get to the place we are today. I have illustrated challenges that leaving the industrial age has created to fully embracing the information and technological age that we are now in.

In the subsequent and final pages, I will illustrate how technology companies and our youngest generation will be the trailblazers that not only continually redefine how we work and communicate, but also how our largest companies evolve to embrace social values and the human emotion of empathy in making decisions.

Today's children and young adults in America and much of the world are the first generation to live in a world that does not know anything but an Internet-connected world. Their innovations will have profound effects on how our corporations and society progress going forward.

The current movement of private entrepreneurs and public companies across all sectors of business to embrace socially positive missions will only grow moving forward. The seeds of growth were planted by technology companies that have been making the world smaller and more connected through improved communication over the past 35 years.

Redefining Public

The founders of technology companies that have gone public over the last three decades have learned many lessons. With each new IPO they have adapted to help keep the founders' vision and empathy intact as they have gone public.

Steve Jobs being ousted as CEO of Apple is probably the most obvious lesson. While in the case of Apple it allowed Jobs to create Pixar and bring an entirely new dimension to Apple upon his return, founders of subsequent technology companies have taken many steps when going public to retain much more control over their innovative businesses to avoid such setbacks.

Tech Embraces Dual-Class Stock

When Google co-founders Larry Page and Sergey Brin took the company public in 2004, they did so in a way that was relatively unique at the time and met with criticism by traditional investment firms. Google offered what is known as a dual-class share structure, which in its simplest definition means that the founders of the company would retain voting control over the company while still benefiting from being able to raise capital through the sale of common stock on a public exchange. Page and Brin took this approach to ensure that their long-term vision for growth was not compromised by shareholder desire for quarterly profits and outlined the reasoning of their motives when filing their registration statement prior to going public.

As a private company, we have concentrated on the long term, and this has served us well. As a public company, we will do the same. In our opinion, outside pressures too often tempt companies to sacrifice long-term opportunities to meet quarterly market expectations...

...If opportunities arise that might cause us to sacrifice short-term results but are in the best long term interest of our shareholders, we will take those opportunities. We will have the fortitude to do this. We would request that our shareholders take the long term view.

Many companies are under pressure to keep their earnings in line with analysts' forecasts. Therefore, they often accept smaller, but predictable, earnings rather than larger and more unpredictable returns. Sergey and I feel this is harmful, and we intend to steer in the opposite direction...

...We are creating a corporate structure that is designed for stability

over long time horizons. By investing in Google, you are placing an unusual long-term bet on the team, especially Sergey and me, and on our innovative approach.

While not new, this model was not often used until Google's IPO. Since then, many technology companies have made similar public offerings.

At least 10 of last year's technology initial public offerings included a special class of shares that give the founders more votes than new shareholders, according to data compiled by Bloomberg. Only five such IPOs were filed in 2010, with four in 2009 and three apiece in 2005 and 2007. In addition to Groupon and Zynga, companies such as Zillow Inc. (Z) and LinkedIn Corp. (LNKD) have embraced the approach.
– Jeff Green and Ari Levy, Bloomberg.com

The latest and most well-known company to follow this trend is Facebook, where founder Mark Zuckerberg will own about 28 percent of the company but hold 57 percent of the company's voting power.

Facebook's structure, like that of Google's and other industry companies, has been criticized by a number of traditional investment firms and Wall Street analysts for taking control away from shareholders. Ironically it is this short-term profit-driven mindset of analysts on investing that our technology corporations are trying to avoid. It also illustrates just how disconnected Wall Street is from understanding exactly how significant this shift is going to change the American economy.

Public companies aren't going to disappear, but we are witnessing a significant shift in power from shareholders to entrepreneurs and managers, one that may make the stock market less central to American capitalism.
– James Surowiecki, The New Yorker

Wall Street, while being rightfully cautious, is fighting a shift in how we may view all public companies in the future, starting with our technology companies today. In a discussion on technology, innovation and the global economy in 2009, Google's Eric Schmidt was asked by an audience member if technology companies would face a social backlash as the industry grows due to concerns about privacy and cloud computing. His response relates well historically to any major change in a technology or economy.

I do believe it's a threat. I believe that most of us are ignorant of history, and we are too stove piped to look at everything correctly. It seems to me that the phenomenon that you're describing has existed in America for hundreds of years. That the rise of every technology has brought people who were naysayers and, in some cases, they were genuinely terrified of it. In some cases they were part of an institution

that was threatened by the rise of the technology, and they were doing their best to delay it. And the reason by-the-way it is so messy is that the incumbents fight tooth and nail against the change because it's in their economic interest to do so; it's not that they're bad people, but they're essentially incentivized to fight progress. What happens is eventually they give up because they retire or their companies go bankrupt or nobody cares anymore.

From our prospective, we believe that the principles of consumer focus, consumer benefit and transparency will ultimately win over the skeptics. This is not an industry that operates in secret. This is an industry that operates in declining costs not increasing costs, and so it's always better next year. Which is a nice message from the stand point of the political operatives and so forth and so on.

So as long as the industry doesn't do anything stupid, I think we'll be just fine.

The idea of consumer focus, consumer benefit and transparency to the user is precisely why the dual-share model is so well suited for technology companies. By retaining controlling ownership of their companies, innovative leaders like Page, Brin, Schmidt, Zuckerberg and Sheryl Sandberg are uniquely suited to weigh equally the needs of shareholders for profits and consumers for privacy and service.

Enter Women

When I began researching the people, stories and companies that would be included in this book in December 2011, I began a serendipitous journey of exploration and learning. Over the following months, I logged countless hours listening, re-listening and internalizing the audio book biography of Steve Jobs; watched countless presentations, commencement speeches, keynote addresses, panel discussions and TED Talks given by Walt Disney, Larry Page, Sergey Brin, Eric Schmidt, Bill Gates, Mark Zuckerberg, Steve Jobs and many others. Digesting all of this material in a condensed period of time has allowed me to see the progression of their ideas over a long period of time, as well as how they appreciate the innovative ideas of their peers.

What was missing, however, would be how women would influence the industry and affect innovation going forward.

It was not until Facebook's IPO announcement that the importance of Sheryl Sandberg came to my full attention. As Chief Operation Officer (COO) of Facebook, she has arguably become the first woman to be in charge of day-to-day operations of a company that by its own definition is setting out to accomplish a social mission — to make the world more open and connected.

I really believe in what Facebook does. You know technology was going to change all our lives, and it has. But technology to power us as people is really the social networking movement. People donate organs, people find their birth mothers, people find friends in ways they never would, and people even start movements. – Sheryl Sandberg, COO of Facebook

Until this point in time the technology revolution, at least at the upper leadership level, has been mostly made up of men. Having a woman running the business operations of Facebook adds an element to Facebook's leadership that is currently rare among corporations.

Prior to joining Facebook in 2008, Sandberg was a research assistant at the World Bank where she worked on health projects in India dealing with leprosy, AIDS and blindness, followed by serving as chief of staff for the United States Department of the Treasury. In 2001 she joined Google as Vice President of Global Online Sales and Operations, as well as being involved in launching Google's philanthropic arm Google.org. Sandberg also serves on the board of directors for The Walt Disney Company, in addition to being a married mother of two.

Sandberg was influenced by parents who had a very deep commitment to doing something for the world, and from that upbringing and her experience until 2001, had always believed she would have a career in government or nonprofits because they make a difference in people's lives. Until Google she never expected to be in the for-profit sector.

At the treasury we would meet with all kinds of people. You get to meet with all kinds of people in the government, and it seemed like what was actually changing people's lives the most to me was technology; and so I wanted to work there, and I kind of had to get over the fact that these were for-profit companies. But I believe they were for-profit companies that were really changing who we were as people and how we interacted, and so I went to Google.

Over the past few years Sandberg has become an outspoken voice for a future where women claim their place as equals in the upper levels of business and men are freely accepted as equals in the home.

A world where men ran half our homes and women ran half our institutions would be just a much better world. – Sheryl Sandberg, 2011 Barnard College Commencement

While Sandberg's position at Facebook has provided a unique platform for her to be outspoken, she is certainly not the only woman shaping the technology industry. Virginia M. Rometty, IBM, and Ursula Burns, Xerox, both serve as the CEOs of those two well established technology companies as capstones to their long careers in technology. Numerous technology and social media startups have been founded by women in the past decade. Marissa Mayer, CEO of Yahoo, was formerly Vice President of Product Management at Google, Google employee number 20, and one of the largest influences on Google's user interface experience. Mayer has a very optimistic outlook on the future for women in technology.

The fact that technology is now so tangible in our everyday lives, I think it will inspire a lot more women to go into technology, and I'm really heartened by that. – Marissa Mayer, CEO of Yahoo

What is exceptional about the technology age and how women are shaping it is that they bring an inherently human element to business and intuitively bring empathy to the direction that corporations and the economy are going.

Connecting Dots and Changing the World

You can't connect the dots looking forward; you can only connect them looking backwards. So you have to trust that the dots will somehow connect in your future. You have to trust in something — your gut, destiny, life, karma, whatever. This approach has never let me down, and it has made all the difference in my life. – Steve Jobs, Stanford University Commencement

A common theme among the innovators of our technology age is their optimistic and long-term view of the future and focus on following your dreams and intuition. While most other industries today are concerned primarily with growth and quarterly profits in a declining economy, the leaders of the technology industry are almost obsessed with following dreams, embracing serendipity, creating social change and making the world more connected in an effort to change society for the better.

When a really great dream shows up, grab it! When I was here at Michigan, I had actually been taught how to make dreams real! I know it sounds funny, but that is what I learned in a summer camp converted into

a training program called Leadershape. Their slogan is to have a "healthy disregard for the impossible." – Larry Page, University of Michigan Commencement

Page's commencement is a moving story of his upbringing and education and how it enabled him to dream big and eventually while working with Sergey Brin, create Google. Page's father, a computer science graduate in 1965, can be credited for Page's interest in technology, transportation and helping society. Page's father Carl was valedictorian of the Flint Mandeville High School class of 1956, and Page included part of his father's graduation speech in his own commencement address.

We are entering a changing world, one of automation and employment change, where education is an economic necessity. We will have increased periods of time to do as we wish as our work week and our retirement age continue to decline.

We shall take part or witness developments in science, medicine and industry that we can only dream of today. – Carl Page

Walt Disney had opened Disney Land only a year before Carl Page's high school graduation and made the following statement when he dedicated Tomorrowland.

Tomorrow can be a wonderful age. Our scientists today are opening the doors of the Space Age to achievements that will benefit our children and generations to come. The Tomorrowland attractions have been designed to give you an opportunity to participate in adventures that are a living blueprint of our future. – Walt Disney

Carl Page likely shared a similar view to Walt Disney about the future promises of technology and shared his many insights and excitement about new things with his son who now is at the helm of one of the most profoundly innovative companies in history.

What is the one-sentence summary of how you change the world? Always work hard on something uncomfortably exciting!

Technology and especially the internet can really help you be lazy. Lazy? What I mean is a group of three people can write software that

CORPORATE EMPATHY

millions can use and enjoy. Can three people answer the phone a million times a day? Find the leverage in the world, so you can be truly lazy!

Overall, I know it seems like the world is crumbling out there, but it is actually a great time in your life to get a little crazy, follow your curiosity, and be ambitious about it. Don't give up on your dreams. The world needs you all! – Larry Page, University of Michigan Commencement

Henry Ford's love of technology and automation influenced Walt Disney. Disney's EPOCT idea and his love of innovation and imagination likely influenced Larry Page's view of the future through his father. Steve Jobs' intuition for new products and ideas brought profound change to multiple industries, and through Pixar, influenced the direction of The Walt Disney Company where Sheryl Sandberg serves as a director today. These innovative leaders did not know that these dots would connect looking forward, but with the depth of connectivity brought on by Mark Zuckerberg's creation of Facebook, these and more technology pioneers certainly can looking back today.

Education

As a person who believes in education, it's obvious that the people who are in education… at the K-12 area as well as the universities, have not gotten… the credit, the attention, the funding, and really the sort of understanding of the role that they play. So we have an opportunity now in crisis to understand what's really important in life, and I would argue that an educated population is the only thing that is important. – Eric Schmidt, Google

Globally every country is currently working to reform public education in an effort to adapt to the new emerging economies being ushered in by the technological revolution. Challenges to true reform are constant and seem to be increasing instead of decreasing.

The current system of education was designed and conceived and structured for a different age. It was conceived in the intellectual culture of the Enlightenment and in the economic circumstances of the Industrial Revolution. – Sir Ken Robinson, PhD

The biggest challenge to education reform is economic. The economic conditions that our current system developed under were based on a linear education process that prepared students for a linear career path. Your professional (academic) or industrial (skilled trade) career path would provide greater opportunities with time as you climbed the ladder of experience for the profession or trade you entered with growing financial compensation to match.

The current student loan bubble and number of "career students" illustrates that people want to learn and expand their intelligence. However, our current education model is too linearly structured and singularly focused on merit-based professions.

I believe we have a system of education which is modeled on the interest of industrialism and in the image of it. I'll give you a couple examples. Schools are still pretty much organized on factory lines. On ringing bells, separate facilities, specialized into separate subjects.

We still educate children by batches. You know, we put them through the system by age group. Why do we do that? You know, why is there this assumption that the most important thing kids have in common is how old they are. You know, it's like the most important thing about them is their date of manufacture. – Sir Ken Robinson, PhD

We currently treat our education system as an economic liability, the cost of which is assumed by students and subsidies provided through taxation. Our technology based economy requires education to be held instead as an economic asset for the country.

Innovations of the technological age in America will occur at our universities where the means of production are educated students, and their ideas will be our exports. Our capitalistic system should treat this new reality like every industry prior, by using competition to lower the cost of production and while creating a superior product to that of competing universities and more importantly in our global economy, other countries.

Turnstile Education

A common theme in conversations and panels by Sandberg, Schmidt, Jobs and Zuckerberg, among many others in the industry, is that our current immigration policy is stifling innovation in our own country. We severely limit the time that foreigners receiving a higher education in our universities can stay in the United States, instead of capitalizing on the innovations and ideas they could be developing for our universities and corporations.

Supporting this policy is the notion that educated foreign workers simply displace Americans at domestic jobs. In addition to a longer-term investment in becoming part of our culture, the actual outcome would be an increase in new innovations that would be owned by American universities and corporations and would lead to more technology-related jobs being created.

We give a huge percentage of the spots in our engineering undergrad and grad program to people from other countries, and then we kick them out. It's like a company; we'd have Facebook training and we train everyone and then we'd say but you can't work here. Go work for our competitor. That's what we're doing as a country. People have talked about stapling. We should be stapling a visa to every high-tech diploma because those people, not only do they not take jobs from other Americans. They create jobs for other Americans. – Sheryl Sandberg, COO of Facebook

The statement above was made by Sandberg in a 2011 interview with Charlie Rose, which she followed with a story of a high-level engineer at Facebook who was able to stay in the United States only because they won a lottery for a work visa. Had he been unable to stay, the jobs under him would have been moved to a foreign country that he could work in.

Generation Empathy

Your time is limited, so don't waste it living someone else's life. Don't be trapped by dogma — which is living with the results of other people's thinking. Don't let the noise of others' opinions drown out your own inner voice. And most important, have the courage to follow your heart and intuition. They somehow already know what you truly want to become. Everything else is secondary. – Steve Jobs, Stanford University Commencement

The current generation of youth are communicating and interacting with more people and information than at any other time in our history. They require an education system that adjusts with them as they explore, evolve, and most importantly, innovate more fluidly than previous generations.

Today's youth and many others who may not be so young in physical age are the first Americans since our country's founding who seem to truly value communication and travel as tools to both explore and experience the world. They want to head out into the world to meet with the people of other cultures to directly learn from them and to share the empathetic spirit that our freedom provides. Unlike the packaged propaganda of yesterday, our young Americas are our best chance for the balanced sharing of information, freedom and innovation throughout the world.

In May 2012 Eric Schmidt gave the University of Boston commencement and shared his thoughts on the bright future that lay ahead for this technology generation.

You have an advantage; you have a competitive edge. You have an innate mastery of technology and ability to find, build and foster connections that no generation before you has ever possessed. It's a very, very powerful skill; that you taught yourself...

For those who say that you're thinking too big, be smart enough not to listen; for those who say that the odds are too small, be dumb enough to

give it a shot; and for those who ask, how could I do that? Look at them straight in the eyes and say, I will figure it out. But above all, be an adorer of life…

This generation will break a new day, your vast knowledge will see the new era, your new ideas will shape a new reality, your agile minds will shape a new dawn. You will give our future a heartbeat and that beat will beat stronger because of you; because of the things you learn and the things that you care about and the values and the things you are going to do.

From my perspective looking at this class, I say that you have the potential to reach higher than any class before you, that any generation that ever came before you. You can reach as high as the face of life itself. – Eric Schmidt, CEO, Google

These are not the statements and ideals of a simple business man driven by profits, but rather the words of a grandfather, father, husband, and more importantly, an innovative human being who feels strongly about the positive future innovation and technology will bring to humanity.

Schmidt's wife, Wendy, serves as president of The Schmidt Family Foundation whose mission is to advance the creation of an increasingly intelligent relationship between human activity and the use of the world's natural resources. This mission will be accomplished by empathetic companies led by an empathetic generation of new leaders and innovators.

SECTION III: INSTILLING EMPATHY

In *Common Sense*, Thomas Paine made an argument for American independence from Britain on a number of points that are relevant albeit different when applied to where we are as a country today.

Paine is critical of the hereditary succession of monarchies because while a person from a previous generation may have been an appropriate leader it did not necessarily mean that his blood line successors would. Our most innovative corporations were set up by innovative and talented individuals who brought unique talents and ideas to their businesses. The CEOs and executives that follow after a leader is gone are often unable to maintain the same trajectory.

Paine also argues strongly as to why it was the right moment in time for America to claim independence. Two things were in good balance to make winning a war with Britain possible. The first was the size of our population which was large enough to form an appropriate army, yet still small enough that the population could unite behind a single cause. Any later in history and various states and groups might not have been willing join the fight. Secondly, we had an abundance of natural resources without going abroad to raise a fleet of ships for a navy.

It is in the same fashion that I argue we are in the right moment to enable our corporate citizens to fully embrace the responsibilities of personhood with the same enthusiasm they have embraced our freedoms and protections.

With social media and the Internet we have a vast communications infrastructure for people to rally around a productive and optimistic cause. In the words of filmmaker Tiffany Shlain, "The Internet in many ways has given the world a central nervous system. What an amazing time to be alive!"

We have all been deluged with gloom and are ready for a solution. Technology will accelerate the capabilities of our devices and the abilities to manage resources at an exponentially rapid pace.

The best part for us as people and users of the Internet is that the message we are spreading is already supported by the founders of the companies that developed the technology to spread the message in the first place.

Moore's Law

The number of transistors incorporated in a chip will approximately double every 24 months. —Gordon Moore, Intel Co-Founder

Moore's Law can be looked at in terms that the power of technology devices will either double in speed or be half the price every two years. This rule has held firm for more than 50 years now, and it is predicted that it will continue for the next 10-15 years. Considering that Moore thought this doubling would hold true for about 10 years following his prediction in 1965, it is likely that as we go further out, the threshold will also do the same, or maybe only slow down, but certainly not stop.

Moore's Law is why the smart phones we have in our hands today hold more computing power then the entire NASA space program did when launching astronauts to the moon. It also means that in the next 15 years we will likely be able to hold all of the world's information in our hands on a single device.

Moore's Law and the technology it has allowed us to create is why, according to Google's Eric Schmidt, we create today as much content as we did from the beginning of time to 2003 every 48 hours.

A Psychological Evaluation of Corporations

America's Constitution created a republic and adopted capitalism as the political and economic systems by which our citizens, government and industries would operate. The freedom this provided allowed America to become the amazing innovative country it is today. During that time we have developed large corporations that are able to manage resources on a much larger scale than individuals or partnerships ever could.

We have given corporations many of the same constitutional protections and rights like personhood and free speech that we ourselves are entitled to. In that sense, capitalism is our child and we are responsible for its growth, development and actions, as well as the values it will operate by.

Preschool: 3-5 Years

Early in American history corporations were highly regulated and typically given very specific charters of what their purpose would be. In this time corporations were very much like preschool children with government playing the role of parent. Corporations did sometimes abuse the rights they had, but regulation would typically work to keep the abuse from being repeated. The overall system, however, allowed innovation to thrive leading up to the Civil War.

Grade School: 5-12 Years

During much of the Industrial Age, corporations were like pre-teen children. Our child was amazingly quick to adapt to new technology and learning but often defiant as it learned how to communicate and negotiate. Our child knows right from wrong but tests the limits of parents and other authority in an effort to find themselves.

It was during this period that unions and trade associations developed to help work with government to make sure that corporations stayed within the boundaries of human rights and the law. It is also the period of time when corporations successfully established themselves with many of the same rights as people using the 14th Amendment, which recognized all people as being protected under the United States Constitution.

High School: 12-18 Years

With the dawn of the technology revolution, American corporations have hit puberty and are going through the turbulent growth phase of adolescence. They are increasingly smart and embracing the exponential growth of technology. Like the average teen, they push the limits of authority as far as they can and only apologize and back peddle when caught.

In this period we have added consumer action like awareness campaigns, consumer reviews and boycotts to assist with keeping corporations in line. The Internet and social media have given consumers the voice they need to share information about companies and build movements to help drive change.

College: Adulthood

The current dramatic love/hate relationship we have in corporate America is very similar to that of a headstrong high school student, manipulating the system to their advantage. Our corporations are also exhibiting characteristics similar to someone with sociopathic tendencies defined as a personality disorder manifesting itself in extreme antisocial attitudes and behavior and a lack of conscience.

With the accelerated growth of technology over the next 10-15 years predicted by Moore's Law, we are in essence about to send our teen to college for their bachelors and masters degrees and likely a doctorate for good measure. Like a college student, corporations must be able to self-regulate their behavior to survive on their own. We can no longer rely on the parenting of government, unions, industry groups and consumers to react quickly enough to the huge jumps in technology and innovation that are ahead of us.

Like Frankenstein's monster, we as a country created and gave rights to corporations and are responsible for their development. A child with sociopathic tendencies who is mistreated by its parents, yet highly intelligent, will oftentimes become a psychopath.

We must push to instill empathy in corporate America to do the right thing in the same way we expect an individual adult.

Finding Purpose

Most businesses exist because a person or group of people came together behind a common goal or idea with the incentive that providing something of value would in turn provide them with a means to profit and earn a living. The value had to be provided before the profit was realized. The legal formation of a corporation has become the best way for a group of people to accomplish this.

A company is really, I think, for a lot of things the most effective vehicle to effect change in the world; because people have all these different goals. The employees who come work at Facebook; a lot of them want to come because it's the best place to engineer and build stuff; other people want to come because their friends use and love the product; other people want to come because they believe in the mission; other people want to come because of someone smart they know is at the company; other people want to come because they want to make money. Right? And none of these reasons are bad, but making it so that you can do all of these things. Make it so that no matter what people's goals are, your organization can attract the very best people to come. I think that gives you the best shot of success.

For-profit companies really give a great ability to align the incentives of a lot of people towards a goal.

Society tends to undersell the mission value that for-profit companies can have. – Mark Zuckerberg, Facebook

For much of the previous 100 years, we have held corporations to a lower standard of operation than we hold ourselves. Much of that is due to government regulation, unions and consumers trying to keep companies in check; to having had each new generation be more prosperous then their parents; to being a world super power while other countries collapsed. Those facts are no longer a reality.

The usual explanation given for the primary purpose of a for-profit company is to make money for shareholders. In the minds of many people that has almost become law. The irony, however, is that it never has in fact been law. The opinion, and in fact it was only an opinion, stems from a 1919 Michigan Supreme Court decision in Dodge v. Ford Motor Co. where the court made an offhand remark that, "a business corporation is organized and carried on primarily for the profit of the stockholders." The opinion was not relevant to the actual ruling and has not been sighted in other court cases since in a relevant manner.

Lynn Stout, Professor of Law from the University of California, Los Angeles (UCLA) School of Law, provides an excellent explanation of why Dodge v. Ford is still taught to law students.

In particular, Dodge v. Ford serves professors' pressing need for a simple answer to the question "What do corporations do?" Their desire for a simple answer to this question can be analogized to that of a parent confronted by a young son or daughter who innocently asks "Where do babies come from?" The true answer to where babies come from is difficult and complex, and can lead to further questions about details of the process that may lie beyond the parent's knowledge and comfort level. It is easy to understand why, faced with this situation, many parents squirm uncomfortably and default to charming fables of cabbages and storks. Similarly, professors are regularly confronted by eager law students who innocently ask, "What do corporations do?" It is easy to understand why professors are tempted to default to Dodge v. Ford and its charming and easily-understood fable of shareholder wealth maximization. – Professor Lynn Stout

Today the emphasis placed on profits above all else is changing dramatically as the leadership and workforce of our corporations becomes younger, more diverse and more gender balanced. Companies like Facebook, as noted by Molly Graham while the head of Culture and Engagement there, "is a company designed by millennials for millennials." The pace of change in corporate culture will increase as more companies disrupt industries outside of their core business and consumers reward and recognize them for doing so.

Betray the Age

In researching and discussing this book, the most common question has been how this change in philosophy and action for corporations would be encouraged. Considering the incentives many industries have to keep things the way they are, I had been unsure until the final months of writing. In the beginning, I was not even sure it was legal.

Never doubt that a small group of committed people can change the world. Indeed, it is the only thing that ever has. – Margaret Mead

Today's "small group of committed people" is really a growing number of public corporations with innovative ideas and leadership committed to changing the world. These companies embrace the freedoms and incentives that capitalism provides a for-profit company while also understanding the responsibility that large corporations, like family businesses before them, have to the community at large.

Companies that have already changed and influenced industries outside of Silicon Valley should be supported in their efforts to continue injecting information age philosophies and economic ideas into other industries. Telecommunications, journalism, recording, television, retail, publishing, and others have already strongly shifted in growing favor of the consumer due to influences from companies outside of those industries.

Apple and Google completely changed our capability expectations for cell phones. Craigslist destroyed the classified business for newspapers, leaving them crippled to catch up with Google and the blogosphere. While the recording industry resorted to suing teens for stealing music, Apple cornered the online music market with the iPod and iTunes and subsequently decimated the brick and mortar retail music industry. Amazon forever changed retail overall and was a significant reason for the failure of Border's Books; while Netflix rendered the video store obsolete and combined with YouTube and other entertainment options is increasingly threatening traditional broadcast media. Further innovative actions by profitable empathetic technology companies into even more traditional industries will continue to push this shift.

Singer Bono during his 2004 University of Pennsylvania Commencement Speech quotes a line from Irish poet, Brendan Kennelly's epic *The Book of Judas*.

There's a line in that poem that never leaves my mind, it says: "If you want to serve the age, betray it." What does that mean, to betray the age? Well to me betraying the age means exposing its conceits, it's foibles, it's phony moral certitudes. It means telling the secrets of the age and facing harsher truths. Every age has its massive moral blind spots. We might not see them, but our children will.

Bono then describes how slavery and segregation were previous moral blind spots overcome by earlier American generations. He goes on to share his love of America because it is not just a country, but an idea; an idea that requires responsibility, equality, and where anything thought of – is possible.

We are a proving ground of new ideas and innovation. The

technology and the information ages are being shaped by the innovative outliers of the Boomer Generation, the innovative early adopters of Generation X, and a majority of value-driven Millennials.

At first the idea of empowering corporations and industries to act with empathy seems foreign, the title of this book an oxymoron. According to Joel Bakan's 2004 book, *The Corporation*, it is not something we can even expect from people as individuals, let alone a corporation.

No one would seriously suggest that individuals should regulate themselves, that laws against murder, assault, and theft are unnecessary because people are socially responsible. Yet oddly, we are asked to believe that corporate persons--institutional psychopaths who lack any sense of moral conviction and who have the power and motivation to cause harm and devastation in the world--should be left free to govern themselves. – Joel Bakan

Besides being published before most millennials reached college and social networking exploded, the statement above has a fatal flaw. We absolutely expect and witness individuals that regulate themselves every day. Laws against murder, assault, and theft are only necessary so that we have a fair and just system of dealing with the relatively few individuals who are not able to carry themselves in a socially responsible manner within society.

The opinion that capitalism and corporate governance must revolve around the exploitative pursuit of profit is a moral blind spot that will be resolved by today's innovative corporations and the boards, shareholders, employees and consumers that support those companies. The same year *The Corporation* was published, Bono gave his commencement address to one of the earliest graduating Millennial classes, and Mark Zuckerberg had just started writing the code that would become Facebook. The gigantic cultural shift created by social media has brought on what author Gary Vaynerchuk in 2011 described as *The Thank You Economy* and has shifted marketing and consumer behavior in a way that is having a dramatic effect on the traditional corporate model.

The world of business is coming full circle. The rise of the Internet and the empowerment of the common consumer has created a fundamental shift in how businesses are expected to behave. – Gary Vaynerchuk, *The Thank You Economy*

Being just a year older than myself, Vaynerchuk has witnessed the same developments in technology and how the information age is shifting corporate behavior as I have. There are a growing number of examples that illustrate how companies and the people leading them understand this shift. While researching this book, it was not until mid-June that I discovered the works of Bakan and Vaynerchuk and subsequently read them along with *Married to the Mouse* by Richard Foglesong that detailed the relationship between The Walt Disney Company and Orlando and Osceola County in Florida.

Foglesong's narrative history of Disney's relationship with the state of Florida published in 2003 is told in the terms of a marriage that goes through stages like serendipity, seduction, growth, conflict, abuse and therapy. Like Florida's relationship with Disney, I believe we have arrived at the therapy phase in our relationship with corporations in general. The open dialogue created by the Internet among the public, as well as with companies, is permanently changing our economic system.

Companies are no longer able to ignore the voices of consumers, employees, staff and shareholders or hide the shortcuts in quality and safety that are taken in order to increase profits. Corporate irresponsibility is quickly becoming a large enough economic liability that proactively making socially responsible and empathetic choices will soon be the more profitable and competitive choice.

Imagine the level of innovation industries would reach if companies actively made better choices for long-term advances. The companies that embrace empathy today will hold a significant competitive advantage over those that continue to pretend that the world is not changing around them.

I am excited that we are a part of this great new age.

NOTES